Curve
Balls
from
Above

Overcoming Adversity to Appreciate Life's Journey

By G.W. Kimmel

Monarch Publishing Group

Changing Our Small World...One Good Book at a Time™

The purchase of this book benefits the Knights of Columbus Council 7736 scholarship funds. For each book sold, $1.00 will be donated to help scholarship recipients attend college.

Library of Congress Control Number: 2014931138
ISBN: 978-0615905020

This books is dedicated to:

Barbara, the light of my life

Karla, Kari, Paul, Ron & Robbie, who have seen me through, and have been the sources of some wonderful and heartwarming times in my life

Lil & Casey Piatek, the very best in-laws a guy could ask and pray for

Father Tony Muldery, my pastor, friend and mentor

Father George Foley, my pastor and dear and close friend

Brandie Mitchell, fellow educator, dear friend and confidant

George and Paula, our closest and dearest friends

Mario Portoundo, my very dear friend who is like a brother to me

Cleta Yancy, fellow educator, friend and mentor

Preface

Have you ever just sat and wondered "Why" certain things in your life turned out the way they did? Do you find yourself questioning some of the decisions you have made and imagine how different things might have been had you not made those particular ones? Do you ever question your faith or ask questions of God as to "Why" certain events did or did not occur in your life?

I have, and they have prompted me to write this book. As a child, and to some extent as an adult, I have always had a wild and active imagination. My imagination has molded me into the fine, upstanding person I am today. It has also helped me deal with the "Curve Balls" that God has thrown my way.

Like all of us, I took it very personal when something disastrous happened in my life. I felt as though no one had ever felt what I was feeling. I felt alone and abused by what life was handing me. After a while, I really don't know when, I came to realize that all people have similar circumstances in their lives. I came to realize that I am not alone in this thing we call life.

I eventually came to realize that no matter what I did, or did not do, that life would go on with or without me in it. I began to look at life as a plan for me that is guided by forces greater than me, and that I should "Go with the Flow" or get off the ride. I realized that we are all going to experience times of triumph and turbulence.

I think we all must realize that our lives are being guided by these special forces. We must come to the realization that in time, God will throw us all some "Curve Balls" and we need to adjust to how we handle them. I have written this book to tell you about some of the "Curve Balls" that God has sent my way and how I adjusted to and accepted them. I can only hope that you may benefit from my experiences and that this book has been as enjoyable to read as it has been to write.

Table of Contents

Chapter 1 .... My Early Childhood
Chapter 2 .... East Street School
Chapter 3 .... I Get a Stepmother
Chapter 4 .... Mc Naugher School
Chapter 5 .... My Perry High
Chapter 6 .... Air Force Basic Training
Chapter 7 .... Basic Medical Training
Chapter 8 .... My First Air Force Leave
Chapter 9 .... Gunter Air Force Base
Chapter 10 .... North to Alaska
Chapter 11 .... Everything's Bigger in
                              Texas
Chapter 12 ....Way Up North
Chapter 13 ....Eglin AFB 1967-1969
Chapter 14 ....The Land of the Rising Sun
Chapter 15 ....California Here I Come
Chapter 16 ....The School of Health Care
                              Sciences
Chapter 17 .... My Final Air Force
                              Assignment
Chapter 18 ....Mustang, Oklahoma
Chapter 19 ....Welcome to Atlanta
Chapter 20 .... Dallas, Texas 1991-1994
Chapter 21 .... Hafa Dai from Guam
Chapter 22 .... Miami 1996 to 2001
Chapter 23 .... Bahama Mama
Chapter 24 .... Deep in the Heart of Houston
Chapter 25 .... Back to Nassau
Chapter 26 .... Houston, the Final Call
Chapter 27 .... Home in Mansfield, Texas

Chapter 1
My Early Childhood

I was born on August 26, 1941, in the year of our Lord, to George Lewis Kimmel Jr. and Lucille Mae Hare (Mr. & Mrs. George L. Kimmel Jr.). My loving parents named me George William Kimmel. The George was in honor of my father and my grandfather. I was told that they changed my middle name to William so that I would not be referred to as "George the third" or "Georgie number three". I guess I can accept that explanation, although there was at least one famous George the Third in history.

My first "Curve Ball" from God came a few days after my birth when He allowed my loving parents to nickname me "Butch". I ask you, who would do that to a beautiful bouncing baby boy such as I must have been? I am over 70 years old and I still have relatives that call me "Butchie". This is really embarrassing for an old, white haired and over the hill guy.

My question has always been, "Why" couldn't they have called me Bill or Billy and used that middle name that they changed? I have two younger brothers who have regular names with no nicknames attached. Over the years, I have accepted this "Curve Ball" and through my wild and active imagination I have made Butch to mean a

My Parents Before They Were Married

"Special", "Handsome", "Bright" & "Unique" being. It works, for God has given me the talents that I possess. My mother was only seventeen years old, and already a mom.

By the time my mother was twenty, she had two more sons, and a lot of responsibility for someone so young. My youngest brother, Bob, was born on August 26, 1944. Yes! He was born on my birthday. Bob was my second "Curve Ball" from God, as I now had to share my "Special Day" with this other person who looked an awful lot like Winston Churchill.

Keep the date August 26th in mind, as it is cause for another one of my "Curve Balls". Over the years, I have forgiven and even "Thanked God" for putting Bob in my life. My dad bragged a lot about having two sons born on the same day, and made it seem as though he planned it that way. Not a chance he did this on his own. It was by the grace of God.

I haven't said much about my middle, and accident prone brother, Jim. Jim has had just about every part of his body in a cast or bandages over the years for being involved in one type of accident or another. There was a time span when he was injured four summers in a row. My dad used to say, "That boy trips over air", as he was always in some state of recovery. Jim was born on December 18, 1942, so you can see that we were really evenly spaced. As I look back at this time in my life, with me and my two brothers, I realize that God had also thrown a "Curve Ball" or two at my parents. The Kimmel Boys were Hell on Wheels and a real handful.

Just after the birth of my brother Bob, my dad was drafted into the Army. The United States was fighting in World War II, and all able bodied young men were being called to Arms. I didn't consider my dad being drafted as a "Curve Ball" because we were at war at the time. My next "Curve Ball" from God happened in 1944 when I was run over by a Coca Cola truck on Shadeland Avenue in the front of my grandfather's barber shop. My Grandmother Kimmel had gotten me a Dixie cup filled with chocolate ice cream, and I had thrown the lid into the street. I realized that the lid had a picture of one of my "Heroes of the Day" on it and I ran into the street to retrieve it. They tell me that my Gran carried me about six blocks to the hospital, and that she cried all the way there. I ended up spending several months in the hospital in traction to prevent one leg from being shorter than the other. It was then that I realized that God had a plan for me and would always be there for me in times of trouble. My dad was sent home on emergency leave from basic training and we were able to see him one more time before he was shipped off to war in the Philippines. I don't remember too much about the war, but do remember how happy I was when my dad came home for good.

My Grandmother Kimmel placed an old Maxwell House coffee can next to my bed at the hospital, and everyone who came to see me put money into this can. Gran Kimmel told me that I could buy anything I wanted just as long as I got well and got out of the hospital. Gran was a very smart lady and really knew how to motivate. There was a bunch of money in that can when I got out of the hospital. I surprised the whole family with what I wanted to buy. "Hello" Tom the duck. I don't know why, but all I wanted was a live baby duck. Back then, pet stores sold colored baby chicks and ducks, and I had my heart set on a blue duck. Being a person of her word, my Gran Kimmel got me a blue duck and I named him Tom. Tom was not allowed in the house, but I had a special place for him on the back porch that was ours.

I walked Tom on a string when he was little and on a chain collar when he got bigger. We went everywhere together, and I loved that duck. My next "Curve Ball" from God came on the Thanksgiving after I got out of the hospital when my family had Tom over, as the "Honored Guest", for dinner. Tom had gotten really big, and the messes he made were bigger than he was. I was devastated and to this day could not eat duck if I were starving to death. God intervened once again and my Grandfather Kimmel, who raised chickens, put me in charge of taking care of the baby chicks. He also gave me a new nickname that only he was allowed to call me. He called me Peep because he said that was the sound that the baby chicks made. I didn't mind it unless someone else called me by it and then I got mad. All three of my sons would learn about this nickname. They would call me Peep behind my back.

My next "Curve Ball" from God came when I turned five years old. I was forced to go to a place called kindergarten. What did I know about this place they called kindergarten? I couldn't even spell it and could hardly pronounce it. All I knew was that it took me away from my mom and placed me with a bunch of five year olds who were all crying, "I Want My Mommy." I cried too, but only because I wanted to fit in with these other kids. God moved in again to prove his wisdom by placing Mary Jane Austin in my life at that time and place. She was my first love, best friend and a person I would always remember fondly. Mary Jane liked to do all of the things I liked to do, and she wasn't afraid to get a little muddy in the process. I often wonder where Mary Jane is now, and how her life may have turned out. I wonder if she thinks about me in the same way.

The very next "Curve Ball" that God delivered was

one of the most difficult to accept. It was one that I blamed myself for over a very long period of time.

When I was six and one half. I didn't know why "The Half" was so important when giving one's age, but it was. My mom went shopping and I didn't see her again until I was seventeen years old.   My grandparents, who were babysitting us for the day, referred to it as the longest shopping trip in history for as long as I could remember. I guess because we were young we didn't dwell on the negative. I really don't remember my mom and dad having arguments and disagreements that would have resulted in her leaving. With that in the back of my mind, I therefore blamed myself for her leaving our family.

I thought that if I had been better behaved that she would have stayed with us, but I now realize that it was not my fault. I think it happened because my parents were so young when they married and started a family.   I think that as they matured they just drifted apart. I do remember when my dad came into my grandfather's house crying and holding my mom's farewell note. The look on his face made my heart ache for him more than for me and my brothers. I always remember that look when I think of my dad, and some of the "Curve Balls" God threw him.

As I grew older, I came to realize that what had happened back then was God's plan for my dad at that time in his life. I think that through the years that my dad never quite got over my mom. He held a special place in his heart until he passed away. Every now and again, I would catch a glimpse of the look he had the day she left and have those same feelings of sorrow for my dad.

After my mom's sudden departure from our lives, things changed and in time the pain and guilt eased on us all. We moved in with my grandparents and lived with them until I was nine and a half. There goes that half business again. At the time, my Uncles Paul and John and Aunts Roma and Anna Mae were still living at home. They more than made up for the love we were missing from the departure of our mother.

After the initial shock of our mom leaving wore off, these were some of the best times of my life. There goes God again working his healing magic. My dad came from a large and very close knit family. All of his brothers and sisters would come to visit every Sunday. I was always surrounded by family at least that one day of the week. In addition, some of my cousins lived within walking distance to my grandparent's house. We all grew up as not just family, but good friends. My Uncle John and Uncle Paul were also very cool and my Aunt Roma and Aunt Anna Mae spoiled us rotten. God, Thank you for them.

I can still remember the great aromas that came from my grandmother's kitchen, as she and my aunts prepared the meals of the day. I can honestly say that during the time we lived with my grandparents, I had three really wonderful cooked meals every day. There were no Wendy's, McDonald's or Burger Kings back then. It's a wonder we all didn't weigh a ton with the way we ate. We always called our grandmother Mum, as she did a great job as the best replacement mother ever. There goes God again working that magic in my life.

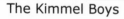 The Kimmel Boys

Chapter 2
East Street School Day

I started East Street Elementary School in the first grade when I was barely six years old. God's next "Curve Ball" was in the form of Mrs. Hedger my first grade teacher. Mrs. Hedger was well over one hundred years old and as mean and nasty as they came, or at least that's how she appeared through my six-year-old eyes. She showed no mercy when it came to math, spelling, reading and all those other things we were supposed to absorb in our six-year-old minds. At the end of each day she would line us up in alphabetical order and check all of our work from that day before she would allow us to leave for the day. If your work was incomplete or incorrect, she would send you back to your seat to complete or correct your work. She would even keep you after the bell had rung and the other kids were outside playing. She certainly was set on us learning. My Uncle John, who was in the fourth grade at the time, was responsible to see that I got home safely every day.

Back then, we actually walked to and from school regardless of the distance. I don't think the school bus had been invented yet. My Uncle John would stand outside my classroom door and pull me out of line when Mrs. Hedger wasn't looking and take me home. He didn't want to wait all day on me or on Mrs. Hedger. I loved my Uncle John. I am not certain, but I think that Mrs. Hedger knew what Uncle John was doing and let it slide. My grades were good and I wasn't the worst behaved kid in class. That title was held by Stanley Behan, who was known as the terror of East Street. I advanced on through to the fourth grade with little to no problems after first grade.

After all, I had survived the likes of Mrs. Hedger.

Today I hold a masters degree in teaching. I can just see Mrs. Hedger taking pride in the part she played in molding my life. Thank you Mrs. Hedger for all you did in my life. East Street School was torn down in the late 70's to make room for a highway and that saddens me.

My dad started dating a woman named Ellen Marie McNemry when I was in the third grade. Ellen was a really cool lady who was really fun to be around. She went on picnics with us, took me to ball games at old Forbes Field and came to Sunday dinners at Gran and Pop's house on a regular basis. She also made my dad happy again. I really liked seeing him with a smile on his face. My dad had a great smile, but he hadn't used it much after my mom left us. I think he blamed himself for us not having a mom around. I didn't realize it at the time, but Ellen was only nine years older than me, so it was no wonder she was fun. My dad must have liked his women young is all I can figure. Ellen would eventually become our stepmother and be involved in several of my future "Curve Balls". Don't get me wrong, she wasn't like the wicked stepmother from Cinderella, but we did have our differences when I was growing up. The key here is that it was all part of life and the process we all go through. God's plan again.

The third grade was also when I experienced what I remember to be my next "Curve Ball" from God. It was Halloween and my Aunt Roma and Aunt Anna Mae decided it would be cute to dress and make me up to be Aunt Jemima of pancake fame. Thank you God for allowing this extreme humiliation to fall upon the nicest nine year old boy on the planet. Aunt Jemima was a somewhat hefty black woman and I was a nine year old pale white boy who was as skinny as a rail. I think back now and I was the first and only cross dresser in my family. On Halloween day at school, it all fell apart in front of the whole school.

My black face makeup kept running from all of the tears I was shedding and my pillow boobs kept falling out of the bottom of my skirt. I was a mess. I don't know how he does it, but God stepped in and turned this embarrassing disaster into a triumphant day. I won the "Best Costume" contest for the whole school and received a Yoyo and a whole box of Bazooka Bubble Gum as first prize. Thank you Aunts Roma and Anna Mae. The remainder of my time at East Street Elementary went well and I had no further "Curve Balls" that are worth mentioning. How could anything top my Aunt Jemima adventure anyway?

Thinking back now, I realize that the years I spent on East Street were some of the best of my life. They have helped to give me my sense of family. We didn't have a whole lot back then as far as material things were concerned, but we certainly did have family. My grandparents, aunts, uncles and cousins saw me through some difficult and crazy times. The time I spent there also gave me an appreciation for the holidays of Easter and Christmas and how important it was to be together during those special days. I still make it a point to be with as much of my own family as possible during the holidays.

East Street School 1945

Chapter 3
I Get a Stepmother

My dad married Ellen Marie McNemry in the summer of 1950 at the home of her parents Charles and Besse McNemry.   Wow! I had two more grandparents to take care of me on my "Shared Birthday", Christmas and other special occasions. It was pretty cool to have an extra set of grandparents. Pop and Gran McNemry turned out to be two of the best people God had put on this earth.   My dad and Ellen were married by a Lutheran minister in the living room in front of the fireplace. My brothers and I attended the ceremony. I can remember my dad having to give the Kimmel boys "The Look" for giggling during the most solemn part of the wedding. We were sorry, but it's not every day that you get to hear your dad say, "I do."

Another "Curve Ball" from God came my way when I learned that we would be moving into a house that was not in the same school district and that I would be leaving all of my friends and cousins behind. Ellen, who we came to call Mom, made my dad happy and that made the move to a new neighborhood tolerable. We moved to 2024 Osgood Street. We would live there until my senior year of high school.   God intervened again and Osgood Street turned out to be a really nice area.   The house on Osgood did, however, start out as a "Curve Ball". It was a three story house and the five of us lived on the third floor for over a year. I had to share a bedroom with both of my brothers and a bed with my accident prone brother Jim.   Would I ever catch a break? I learned how to swim during the year I spent sleeping with Jim.

We had to share the bathroom with the family who lived on the second floor. That made a total of nine people for one bathroom. Talk about waiting to pee and to take care of the other emergencies that arose.

I was a really bashful lad at that stage of my life. I had real nightmares about someone walking in on me in the bathroom and seeing my "Boyhood". I really didn't have a "Manhood" at age ten. However, before anyone had the opportunity to walk in on me, God intervened. The family on the second floor moved out and we now had the second and third floors. Now only five people to use the bathroom. I got my own room and no longer shared a bed with my brother Jim. Jim had a bit of a moisture problem at the time, and there were mornings when I awoke quite damp.

Our parents both worked at the time, so me and my brothers were left on our own from after school until the folks got home from work. The Kimmel boys could really come up with things to do, but for the most part, stayed out of trouble. By then, we had made a few friends and would play ball, skate or ride our bikes until we heard the whistle. My dad and my Grandfather Kimmel had a whistle that could be heard over several counties. It was our signal to come home. I have tried "The Whistle", but it has ended with my generation. I don't know how we did it, but we survived without cell phones, iPods and all that other stuff that prohibit communication between people. We did have Party Line phones and my mom got a lot of good recipes from listening in on someone during a party line conversation. Later on, I met a couple really cute girls through the Party Line. We really didn't need to text back then, as we actually spoke to one another.

We also had a great apple tree in the backyard,

and Mrs. Jordan, our next door neighbor, would bake us pies from those apples. What great times those were. Mrs. Jordan also had a dog named Rusty who really thought he was one of us. Rusty was in the middle of everything we did as kids. I think of him as my first pet, even though he belonged to Mrs. Jordan.

Mrs. Jordan could hardly walk, let alone run, so Rusty needed us to get his exercise. I think back and Rusty is probably the reason I have always wanted and had pets around. I thank God that all of my kids are the same way when it comes to animals. They have all had a variety of pets during their lifetimes. Those pet stories and others will come later.

Ellen turned out to be a pretty good Stepmother. She really loved us a lot. You must remember that she was really young and had taken on a tremendous responsibility by marrying my dad. She walked into a ready-made family of a husband and three boys who had been spoiled rotten by aunts, uncles, cousins and grandparents. I think that people were always trying to make things up for the loss we suffered when our real mom left us. We were a real handful, especially for someone as young and inexperienced as our Ellen. She learned, we adjusted and had a pretty good life on Osgood Street.

My next "Curve Ball" from God is one of the earliest that I remember being delivered by Ellen. When she and my dad married, she had ZERO cooking skills, but was eager to learn and experiment. She made candied sweet potatoes one day from a recipe she had gotten from a magazine. She burned them and the Kimmel boys laughed. Laughing was a gigantic error on our part, as she made us eat them. I didn't look at, or touch, another sweet potato for thirty years and then only when God told me it was okay.

Over the years, Ellen turned into a really great cook. Her meals were on a par with Grandma Kimmel's. I have always had a bit of a sweet tooth and Ellen was always making really great cakes, cookies and other delightful things. I remember one day she made salmon patties that looked like cookies and tasted wonderful. My brother Jim hated fish with a passion, but loved these because they didn't look like fish. Jim has always been a little weird at the table and to this day will not eat a cooked vegetable.

Decisions, decisions, decisions. Not all "Curve Balls" are negative. Some can be downright perplexing. My next "Curve Ball" from God came shortly after we moved to Osgood Street in the form of Dottie Wright and Dana Corbit. Like me, Dana lived on Osgood Street a few houses down and Dottie lived on the corner of Osgood and Lafayette Street. Dottie's house was between mine and Dana's. They were both absolute dolls and both had slight crushes on yours truly. This was the first and I think only time in my life that I had the two girls at once dilemma. Dana was my age and would be in the same grade and homeroom when school started and Dottie was a year younger than us. I would be going to the fifth grade with Dana and Dottie would be in the fourth grade at the same school. What's a guy to do when faced with the two beauty dilemma?

I knew that I would be forced into a decision by this dynamic duo sooner or later and must work out a game plan. Do I follow in my father's footsteps and go for the younger girl, or go with the older woman? Remember, we were nine and ten respectively and really didn't know all that much about the boyfriend/girlfriend do's and don'ts anyway. Again, I was saved by fate. The choices were made for me. Dana ended up with Billy Bastle from church and

Dottie ended up with my brother Jim, of all people. I have seen both Dottie and Dana since our days on Osgood Street and we all laugh about those days.

That first summer on Osgood Street would also bring Colman Conley, Jack and Ronnie Hess, Dave Meals and Dennis Mawhinney into my life forever. Jack, Ronnie and Coleman were all guys from the neighborhood. We spent that first summer and many summers after that doing guy stuff. Jack was into model planes. We would fly and sometimes crash them in front of Jack's house. He was a real craftsman and the planes were a work of art.

Ronnie raised Carrier Pigeons and always smelled a little like bird doo-doo. He loved those birds. They were a thing of beauty as they flew to his signals. Coleman became one of my very best friends over that summer and we still keep in touch today. We still call and email each other often and keep each other up to date on what we are doing. I make it a point to visit with him any time I go to Pittsburgh. I remember the time we took a couple of my mother's cigarettes and were smoking them behind Coleman's garage. We wouldn't let him try it, so he ratted us out to our dad. I can still see and hear him as he stood in the middle of our backyard yelling up to an open window. He yelled, "Hey! "Butch's dad", Butch, Bob and Jim are smoking behind my garage."

He ran home before I could beat the crap out of him. I forgave him and we laugh about that every time when we get together.

My dad was waiting for us when we got back home. He had a fresh pack of cigarettes and some matches ready for us. He made us smoke the whole pack and man were we sick from it. My dad was a "Real Man" and he smoked unfiltered Lucky Strike Cigarettes. These were the most potent of all at the time and really made us turn different shades of several colors when we smoked them.

I met Dave and Dennis at Riverview Park pool where the kids liked to hang out. We became friends that summer and we have been close friends ever since. I don't know why they called it Riverview, as it was buried deep in the heart of the park and all you could see were trees. The three of us went there at least a couple of times a week and had a great time. It was a public park that was run by the city. It was very well maintained. Back then, we didn't worry about some of the types of "Bad Guys" we have today. Kids could just go places and have fun. Like me, both Dave and Dennis had brothers to contend with and that really bonded us. Dave received a really nasty "Curve Ball" that summer when his dad died suddenly of a heart attack. Dave was only nine or ten at the time and his dad was really young. Heart problems must run in Dave's family, as Dave has had three bypass surgeries and his big brother Max has had two. We all played ball together and I thought that we would all just always be healthy.

My next "Curve Ball" from God came at the end of that first summer as we were preparing to start our new school. Our very new and inexperienced stepmother took us shopping for new school clothes and nearly started World War III in the process. Back in the early fifties, life and clothing were very simple and this woman was hell bent on changing all of that. We wore Levi jeans that were ALWAYS two to three inches too long, so that they could be rolled up at least two folds. We also wore plain white t-shirts with the sleeves rolled up to show off our non- existent muscles.

My brothers and I would all be attending the same school and our new and inexperienced stepmother thought it would be "Cute" to put us in matching OUTFITS from head to toe. Her idea of outfits was a kind of dress pants and some kind of plaid flannel shirt with your cool white t-shirt as underwear. We all thought that Ellen was from Mars or someplace that didn't have to worry about how they looked on the first day of school.

This woman was trying to get us killed and have our dad all to herself. Could you just see the three "New Kids" showing up on the first day of school in matching outfits and what we would have gone through? As the "New Kids", you always wanted to maintain a very low profile until you got the lay of the land. This woman had her mind set on putting us on display. Thankfully, our dad and God intervened. We were allowed to pick out our own style of school clothes. We didn't have designer clothes back then and getting us ready for school didn't cost my dad an arm and a leg. The most expensive part of my clothes back then were my Keds sneakers that cost about two dollars at the time. I saw a pair the other day that were almost like what I wore as a kid and they cost eighty dollars on sale. Don't you just love how we have progressed?

The House on Osgood Street

Mrs. Jordan's house is on the right, and the Hillen's house is on the left. The old apple tree is gone.

Chapter 4
Mc Naugher School

Our new school was one and a half miles from our house on Osgood Street. We walked to and from it every day. As I stated earlier, I don't think that the school bus had been invented yet and everybody walked to school or were driven by their parents. I was tasked by my parents to see that Bob and Jim arrived safely every day. The last thing a guy wanted was to be tied down by little brothers and on some days I would pretend that I didn't even know them. Going to school was the easier of the two trips as it was all downhill, but going home was a chore. Bob could keep up pretty well going to school, but we almost had to carry and drag him back home on the uphill portion of our daily journey. I can still hear him saying, "I'm going to tell dad that you dragged me up the hill." He would say that we threatened to leave him. He was after all, the baby of the family and he played that card every chance he got. Bob turned out to be a truck driver like my dad and he reminds me a lot of my dad when he smiles. He can also drink as much beer as the old man, when he wants to.

Fifth grade was a great grade at Mc Naugher School, as Mrs. Palmer was our homeroom teacher. Mrs. Palmer was a great teacher. She was a person who believed in the sugar vs. vinegar method of getting students to work hard. I don't think this woman ever said a cross word or had a bad thought about anyone she came in contact with. Believe it or not, but back in those days we could actually read and enjoy the bible in public school. Mrs. Palmer read to us from hers every morning for the whole first period.

My love for the story of Ruth comes from hearing it first from the lips of Mrs. Palmer. She did the unthinkable and actually made us look forward to going to school.

I don't know how she did it, but she stopped her story each day at some really critical "Tell Me More" point. We were excited to get back the next day just to see how things turned out. She also taught English and writing skills and I excelled in both at that time. My writing has suffered over the years. I used the typewriter when I was in college and the computer these days.

My fifth grade "Curve Ball" from God came in the form of Ms. Leslie, our music teacher. Ms. Leslie was a really old and never married lady who always smelled like onion soup to me. We had Ms. Leslie's class just before lunch and she would be cooking her onion soup on a hot plate during our class. She ate it at least five days a week that I knew of, so naturally she came to smell like and remind me of onion soup. My curve ball from her came on the very first day of music class, when she assigned me to play the TRIANGLE. I had my heart set on banging away on the drums. I thought that the Triangle was a SISSY instrument that should only be played by very weak girls. I loved music and was excited about having a class devoted to it, but now my dreams were shattered. God intervened once again and taught me that the Triangle was a percussion instrument like the drums and I became quite good at it. I could make it sound like rain drops or footsteps depending on the piece we were playing. I learned to love the sounds I made. Later in life, I would get my opportunity to play the drums in both my high school bands and orchestras, but will always fondly remember my days with Ms. Leslie and the Triangle.

Dennis Mawhinney moved away at the end of fifth grade and I would not see him again until high school. He was part of the Three Musketeers of me, Dave and him. Now Dave and I would be just the two Musketeers. That doesn't even sound right and it didn't feel right either.

Mc Naugher also introduced me to sports in a big way. It had a first class gymnasium and an olympic size swimming pool. Coach Lang was our Physical Education teacher. Mr. Jordan (Coach) was our swimming teacher and swim team coach. I swam on the Junior Varsity Swim Team in the fifth and sixth grades and the Varsity Swim Team in the seventh and eighth grades. My stepmom lost all of my medals and ribbons in one of my parents many moves.

In my day, the teachers were allowed to punish students without going to jail and I got a butt whipping from Coach Lang one day that placed a lasting memory on me. Dave, Don Monte and I were cutting up while the coach was explaining something to the class. He had us bend over and touch our toes. I could actually do that back then. He gave us each a whipping that sent us across the gym. I never wanted to cry so bad in all my life, but couldn't. You had to suck it up and be cool. Don Monte told me later that Coach Lang hit harder than his dad. Remembering what that swat felt like, I never did anything else wrong in Coach Lang's class again.

In the sixth grade, new and wonderful things started to happen. I had my very first REAL girlfriend, learned how to dance (mostly the Box Step), got on the Safety Patrol and got my very first paying job. My next "Curve Ball" from God was delivered while I was actually trying to do a big favor for Dave. Loretta Cape, a new girl, had come to our school in the sixth grade. Dave instantly fell in love with this dark haired beauty. Dave was a little on the bashful side. He needed my romantic, match-maker help and nicely asked me to ask Loretta if she liked him and would she go to the next school dance with him. Well, as it turned out, Loretta was going to ask one of her girlfriends to ask me the same thing. Oh, woe is me. How do I break this kind of news to Dave? God stepped in and saved the day with the arrival of the Ritchie twins. Dave fell in love, AGAIN, with both of them and forgot all about Loretta. Loretta taught me how to KISS. Man, did I like it and got rather good at it according to her. Loretta and I lasted through all of sixth grade and broke up over the summer when she fell for Sal Mamaux. I was devastated for about two weeks after that.

I also learned how to dance the Box Step in the sixth grade. We were taught by the girls' and boys' gym teachers during gym class that year. I had always liked music and was growing a fondness for the opposite sex, so dancing was the next logical step. As I remember it, all of the boys in the sixth grade wanted to dance with Margie Schniederlochner, as she was the Goddess of the Orlon sweater. Trust me, all we did at that stage in our young lives was look. We had a school dance for the sixth grade the first Friday of every month and we were always scrambling to see who we could get to go with us. I had a really big crush on Judy Mecky and asked her several times to different dances. She and I met at our 45th high school class reunion and in front of my wife and her husband, we both admitted to the crushes we had on each other at the time. This was the first reunion I had been able to attend. It amazed me how many of these people I still remembered. It, once again, made me realize how really great the life God had given me was. I had a new appreciation for his plan for me.

Every boy in the school wanted to be a member of the Safety Patrol and I was no exception. Coaches Lang and Jordan were the teachers in charge and made all of the selections for it. I was a pretty good athlete and except for the one swat from Coach Lang, I was a model citizen. These were the qualities that they looked for in their selection process. There were four boys selected from each grade level and the odds of making it were slim to none. I don't think that I ever prayed as hard as I did the night before selections. The names were posted during lunch the next day and I had made it. I did remember to thank God, for even back then, I knew I didn't do it on my own.

I served on the Safety Patrol for the remainder of my time at Mc Naugher, and was selected as one of two Lieutenants in the sixth and seventh grade and as Captain of the Safety Patrol in the eighth grade.

"Extra! Extra! Read All About It!" was the battle cry for all good paperboys. Back in my day, people got their news and other information by reading the daily newspaper and not by turning on CNN. There were two newspapers in Pittsburgh at the time and I ended up working for both at age eleven. I sold the Pittsburgh Post-Gazette on the corner of Marshall Avenue from five every morning, seven days a week, until school started. I still remember my dad stopping for his FREE paper every morning on his way to work. I delivered the Pittsburgh Press door to door after school to end my days. I didn't make a lot of money back then, but I did always have a jingle in my pocket. I think that these two jobs and seeing my dad go to work every morning helped to develop my good work ethic. At a point in my life I will discuss later, I had a job I held for six years and never took a sick day. I can still hear my dad saying, "If you can get your head off the pillow, you should get your butt to work." That still applies to me today. Thank you dad.

Here is my sixth grade class picture. I am in the middle of the front row.

Seventh grade was as good as the sixth for me and I can't recall any really bad "Curve Balls" during those years. The one that comes to mind is that all of the girls God put in my life at this time were named Barbara. I went steady with three different Barbara's over that two year period. Who knew at that time that I would later marry a girl with that very name? My Barbara will come along later in this book. My wife teases me when I call her Honey and says that I only do it because I can't remember her real name. This was also a time in my life that I would have some friendships with girls on a strictly girl/boy friend relationship. I had and still have several friends from those days who still communicate with me through email who are just good friends. Jan McMonigal is one of my really good friends who happens to be female. Jan and I loved to cut up and be the class clowns and were always on some teacher's sh*t list for disrupting a class. Jan married her high school sweetheart and they are still happily married after all this time. We still cut up any time we meet.

Eighth Grade Picture

I really got involved in music in the eighth grade. I played both the flute and the drums. I think that I was trying to be my own "Fife & Drum Corps". My next "Curve Ball" from God came with a little bit of an international flair. The eighth grade decided to put on a show for our parents and teachers in order to showcase our musical and dance talents. I was chosen to do the Mexican Hat Dance with a girl I really didn't care for and she **REALLY** disliked me. We had to dress all in black and dance around a Sombrero in front of everyone and I could not get my heart into it. There were a couple of times at rehearsal that I really threw my dance partner around. I hoped that I could control myself on the night of the show. There were four couples who were going to be featured in this dance and one half of each couple did not have their hearts into it. That would be the guy half. On the night of the show, the mother of my dance partner brought really brightly colored sashes for all of the guys to wear as part of our costumes and we all thought that they made us look like a pack of big sissies.   Mine was bright orange, as I recall and it really made me stand out. I could just hear some of my guy friends saying "Nice Sash Mary Jane" or words to that effect. The good Lord intervened and on the night of the show we were a huge success. The brightly colored sashes gave us a kind of Latin flair. We were one of the big hits of the show. I understand that the class behind us did the same thing the following year and that guys and girls were fighting to be selected to do our dance.

The next and last big event for me was my graduation from good old Mc Naugher School. My Grandparents McNemry bought me my very first suit for the occasion and I was really dressed to kill. I was happy to be moving on to high school, but a little sad to be leaving the school that had seen me through some really great times.

At the time of publication, Mc Naugher is up for sale. I hope that whomever buys it will appreciate the history hidden in her halls and walls.

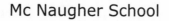

Mc Naugher School

Chapter 5
My Perry High

After graduation from Mc Naugher Public School, I started high school at Perry High School. Back then we were called the Perry Commodores in honor of Commodore Perry. I was only fourteen years old when I entered Perry and was small and really young looking. My next "Curve Ball" from God came on my second day of high school in the form of Max Meals, Larry Meals, Rich Roach and two other seniors I didn't know. I was given my initiation into high school by these five senior boys, as was the tradition for ALL incoming freshmen both male and female. These guys stuffed me into a rolling laundry hamper and wheeled me into the women teacher's bathroom. I remember the ride very well and remember saying "Hello" to Miss Simone who was sitting on the toilet as I sailed through.

I had Miss Simone for Freshmen Latin and she could never quite look me in the eye after that day. God intervened again; I received A's from Miss Simone in that class and Senior Latin three years later. I guess she always remembered that day too. The one great thing about initiation was that it only happened to you once and then you were safe forever. We really didn't have the kinds of bullying problems that today's students face. Our initiation was a fun and funny way the seniors had for welcoming new students to Perry.

My next "Curve Ball" from God came on my first day of band. I was a really good drummer by the time I entered high school. I had dreams and aspirations of playing in the school marching band. Mr. Ambrits, our band director, had other plans for the new rookie band members. He assigned me to play the cymbals and he was dead set on me playing them. I tried my very best to play them, but they were very heavy to carry for a little guy with toothpicks for arms. I only lasted one formal session on the cymbals and then I was promoted to the snare drum section. I ended up playing with both the marching band and the orchestra for my whole four years in high school. Mr. Ambrits was an okay guy and a fantastic musician, but he had absolutely no sense of humor whatsoever. One day he was shouting, "Give me a trill" for the clarinet section, when a voice from the drum section, that sounded like mine, shouted, "Bend over."

The whole band cracked up with the exception of Mr. Ambrits.   He   sent   me   to   see   **MISTER SUTHERLAND.**   Mr. Sutherland, Jock as he was known behind his back, was the man who doled out punishment for what he called "Wiseguyism". I spent one hour after school in detention for three straight days. The rule behind "Wiseguyism" was not to be one at the beginning of the week, but to be one later in the week like Wednesday or Thursday. Mr. Sutherland would always put you in detention for the number of days that were left in the week unless you did something really bad.

My next "Curve Ball" from God was my Uncle Lou's fault and I was an innocent bystander. Every one of my aunts, uncles and cousins attended Perry High School before me. Some had left good impressions, while others left less desirable ones. On my first day of Freshman English, Miss Boggs, the teacher, was taking attendance to see who we were. When she called my name, she asked if I was related in any way to Louis Kimmel. I proudly announced that he was my Uncle Lou and that I worked for him after school. As it turned out, my Uncle Lou was in no way one of Miss

Boggs' favorite students from the past.

She was determined to make me pay for the error of his ways. My Uncle Lou, not only gave me my first job, but was like a second father to me at that point in my life. I kind of forgave him for what Miss Boggs put me through. I was a really good student, and she ended up giving me good grades. To this day, I can only imagine what my Uncle Lou might have been like in her classes.

In addition to Miss Boggs for English, Mr. Ambrits for band and Miss Simone for Latin, I also had Miss Troberts for homeroom, Dr. Irons for biology, Mr. Leggit for history and Mr. Burke for algebra. It seemed that my Uncle Lou had also blazed his trail through some of these teacher's classes, as I heard comments from several of them regarding his behavior.

Algebra was my favorite class at that time, as it introduced me to Mary Grace Elliott. Mary had just recently broken up with Al Brachalili and was a free woman (GIRL).

I had known Mary from our days at Mc Naugher, but did not know her very well. We began talking before algebra class. She sat right in front of me and BINGO we hit it off. Mary was cute, had a great figure and was fun to be around. She seemed to like me a lot and we started going steady shortly after our first date. I had this great steady girl, a great job and was in high school. How good could it get?

This phase of my life with Mary would also introduce me to SEX and according to Mary Grace Elliott I became very good at it. Just as I had in my kissing experience with Loretta Cape. My introduction to sex, ironically came on Good Friday in 1955. Yes! I was only fourteen. I didn't have to be at work that day until noon, so I went over to Mary's house to spend the morning with her. Shortly after I arrived, Mary excused herself and went upstairs to fetch something. She called for me to help her and I went up the stairs where she had gone. Mary called to me from one of the bedrooms. I followed the sound of her voice. When I entered the room, Mary was lying in her bed completely naked. I was dumbfounded, petrified and excited all at the same time. She was the very first girl I had ever seen in that state of undress. The very sight of her took my breath away.

Mary introduced me to the art of love making on that Good Friday morning. I have spent the rest of my life attempting to improve my skills and techniques in that arena. Some years later, the movie "The Jerk" would come out and after seeing it I would always relate to Steve Martin when he came to the realization about what his "Special Purpose" was to be used for. I feel the same way about what happened to me on that Good Friday so long ago.

My next "Curve Ball" from God came a few months later when Mary grew tired of me and was ready to move on. She dumped me for an older guy, Bob Bellis, who owned and drove a brand new fire engine red Oldsmobile convertible.

I was devastated and was certain that life as I knew it was coming to an end. Time and the good Lord saw me through this terrible time in my life. Mary became pregnant a few months later and was forced to leave school and marry this other guy. I can't imagine what turns my life might have taken if that had happened when I was dating her. Thank you God for not letting it happen. From what I learned, they had a baby girl, but did not live happily ever after. They divorced about the same time we were graduating from high school. I guess that was Mary's "Curve Ball".

After Mary dumped me, I didn't have another steady girlfriend until my senior year at Perry. I think that I might have been afraid of being hurt again and did not get close to any one girl for a very long time. Don't get me wrong, I was far from being a hermit, but I was also very careful about opening what I came to refer to as "The Hurt Door" again for a long time.

During this phase of my life, I also worked every day after school and on the weekends for my Uncle Lou. I learned how to cut meat and became a pretty decent butcher by the time I finished high school. I kept my butchering skills unknown when I joined the Air Force, as I didn't want to spend my time working in a commissary somewhere.

Looking back, I started my first paper route when I was eleven and have held a steady job of one kind or another for more than sixty years. I am still a substitute teacher for my local school district and don't know what I might do next. In addition to learning the skills necessary to be a meat cutter, I also developed my customer service skills and learned how to deal with people while working for my Uncle Lou. These would all help me later down the line.

My next "Curve Ball" from God came while I was working for my Uncle Lou and it was in the form of the daughter of one of my Uncle Lou's best customers. One Saturday morning, this really good customer invited me to attend the birthday party of his daughter for that very Saturday night. I had a date with another girl that I was interested in and no desire to spend my Saturday night at a birthday party for some girl I barely knew. Before I had a chance to say anything, my Uncle Lou accepted the invitation on my behalf. Thanks a lot Uncle Lou.

Business was business after all and my Uncle Lou was determined to keep one of his best customers happy at my expense. I pouted all day. I was really angry with my uncle for putting me in this predicament. I did make him buy the birthday present for this girl and pay for my gas for the trip to and from her house. Gas was, after, all .28 cents a gallon and it would cost me about $3.00 to fill my dad's car. I did have to break the date with the other girl. It cost me any future chance I had with her. Boy! Did Lou owe me one for this sacrifice? As always, God stepped in to save the day. I had a great time at the birthday party of Miss Beverly Hines. Beverly turned out to be one of the nicest and sweetest girls I have ever known. We dated off and on until I joined the Air Force. She and her mom both wrote me letters and sent me care packages when I was stationed in Fairbanks, Alaska a few years later.

My next "Curve ball" from God came during the summer before I started my senior year at Perry. My folks decided to move from Osgood Street to Brighton Place to be nearer to my Grandparents McNemry. This house was not in the same school district and I just knew that I was going to be required to change schools going into my final year. What a BUMMER. Once again, the good Lord came to my rescue. The school administrator at Perry gave me a waiver based on the fact that I was a senior and that I had transportation to and from school. With the help of my parents and Uncle Lou, I was able to purchase a 1949 Chevy four door coupe. It had a three speed column gear shift and ran great. It looked really ugly, but it was all mine. My having to change schools problem had been solved. Thanks Uncle Lou, mom and dad for the help and support you gave me.

The house on Brighton Place was a nice three story, four bedroom, three bath house that met our family's needs quite well. It did, however, move me quite a distance from all of my friends from school. We moved into this house on a Friday and I was in a foul mood about having to leave the house on Osgood Street after so many years. God stepped back into my life's big picture the next day and delivered me an angel.   On Saturday morning, I decided to do a "Recon" of the neighborhood and stopped short at the house next door. Edna Mae Dailey was standing on a chair washing her mother's living room windows and she stopped me dead in my tracks. She was wearing shorts and one of her brother Jack's sweatshirts that was at least two sizes too big for her. She had auburn red hair, blue eyes and a smile that immediately took my breath away. I smiled and waved back. That was the beginning of a romance that would last for almost three years.   Eddie, as she was called, was my girlfriend from that day until Christmas Eve of 1961, when we became engaged. My "Curve Ball" from her will come later in this book, but God will once again intervene and make it all better. This was one of the happiest times of my life as I recall. I had a great job. I was in my senior year of high school. I had what could almost be described as a car and I was going steady with "The Girl Next Door". Eddie had two older sisters and an older brother. Her brother and I would become good friends. My days were spent in school, at work and with Eddie every evening and on the weekends. She also worked and I would pick her up every day when she finished. We did all of the Friday night school dances and Saturday nights at the drive - in movies.   Our families also got along great and Eddie's dad and mine became very good drinking buddies. They went to the corner tavern, Moe's Place, almost every night.

I suffered what I like to call one of my most embarrassing "Curve Balls" on the night of my graduation from high school. We had a very large graduating class and our ceremony was held in Carnegie Hall in downtown Pittsburgh on June tenth, 1959. I remember hearing my name being called from the podium. As I walked across the stage to accept my diploma, my cousin Buddy, age four, called out **very** loudly, "There's Butch."

Very few of my classmates and none of my teachers knew my nickname, but they all did after Buddy's outburst to the whole world. I was happy that they made this embarrassing discovery on graduation night and not earlier in my high school career. I do remember, like it was just yesterday, the laughter that came from the audience, my classmates and teachers as I crossed the stage.

Perry High School

Perrysville Avenue
Pittsburgh, Pennsylvania

My Senior Picture

I am only five foot nine, but was six one
with the way I did my hair back then.

During our senior year, we were approached by recruiters from all branches of the military. I had made my mind made up to join the United States Marines. Eddie's older brother Jack was in the Air Force and he was stationed really close to home. Columbus, Ohio was only a three hour drive. Eddie decided that I should join the Air Force like her big brother.   This became a really sore spot in our relationship and she finally laid down the ultimatum that I join the Air Force like her brother or find a new girlfriend.   Being the "Love Sick Fool" that I was, I caved in and enlisted in the United States Air Force. I did all of the paperwork, took all the tests, filled in all of the required boxes on a multitude of forms and was ready to go.

My next "Curve Ball" from God came when my recruiter realized that I was only seventeen and would require the signatures of my father and natural mother. There was an opening and I could go into the Air Force right after graduation. The alternative was to wait a few months until I would turn eighteen. I have always been extremely focused and once I make up my mind to something there is no changing courses for me. I was determined to enter the Air Force at the earliest possible time. Damn age requirement.   Once again, those forces which have always guided my life, stepped in and saved the day. It just so happened that my cousin Nancy was getting married and my mother would be attending the ceremony. Nancy was a cousin on my mother's side of the family. We all went to Nancy's wedding and I met my mother for the first time in all those many years. Remember, she left us when I was six and a half. I didn't recognize her and remember asking my cousin Sonny which one of the ladies was my mom. I approached and spoke to her and we both hugged and cried a little. She was a really beautiful lady. She had re-married and had a husband, a son and a daughter. After explaining my problem to her, she agreed to meet me and my dad at the recruiters on Monday morning.

God really does work in mysterious ways, as he joined my dad, mom, stepmom and my mom's husband together as friends. The four of them became really good and close friends after Nancy's wedding. They got together on many occasions and visited each other when they could. It took a long time, but the old wounds were being healed. I would also visit with my mother and her family a few times when I was changing duty stations.

Chapter 6
Air Force Basic Training

Having met all of the paperwork and physical requirements, I swore "To defend the Constitution of the United States of America against all enemies foreign and domestic" on August 20, 1959. It was just six days before my eighteenth birthday. It would turn out to be a birthday I would always remember.

I remember saying my good-bye's to my dad and stepmother over breakfast that morning. After breakfast, I went and said my good-bye's to Gran and Pop Kimmel, along with my aunts, uncles and cousins. I then stopped by my Uncle Lou's meat market to see him one last time before I left for basic training. He had become like a second father over the years and saying good-bye to him was one of the most difficult things I did that day. My final stop, before going to the main post office, was to say good-bye to Eddie. We held hands, kissed, cried and promised to write every day or as much as we could. We both lived up to that promise and at mail call, I was very rarely disappointed.

After checking in at the post office, we were given our files and put on a bus for the airport. I had never flown before. I was scared "spitless". I did, however, reason that I was going into the Air Force and that this would be my major mode of transportation and that I had better get accustomed to it. Back in 1959, most of the commercial planes were propeller driven and stops were frequent. We departed Pittsburgh in the early afternoon and flew to Birmingham, Alabama on the first leg of our journey. From Birmingham, we next stopped in New Orleans and stayed there overnight. I had not traveled anywhere to speak of, up to this point in my life, so a night in the "Big Easy" really fascinated me.

I was too young and really looked it, to partake of any alcoholic beverages or go into any of the bars on Bourbon Street. I did poke my head into a few places and was fascinated by the sights and sounds. Boy! This Air Force life is really great, as I had already taken my first plane ride and visited one of the most famous cities in the world on my very first day of active duty.

The next morning at around nine o'clock, we boarded the plane for the final leg of our journey. We arrived in San Antonio, Texas around noon on August 21, 1959. When they opened the doors on the plane, I thought we had landed on the surface of the sun. It felt like it was well over the boiling point and that we were all going to melt. I came to learn that the average temperature in San Antonio in August is usually a little over a billion degrees Fahrenheit.

We had a few hot summers in Pittsburgh, but nothing like what I felt when I got off that plane. I thought I had walked into one of the blast furnaces at U.S. Steel. Now that I am older, I actually like the heat on these old bones of mine.

The first sound I heard when I got off the plane was the **thundering bellow** of Master Sergeant Charles M. Story, telling us to, "Fall in ladies."

Fall in? I hadn't been to sleep for a whole day plus some. All I wanted to do at that moment was to fall asleep. We were then herded onto a couple of Air Force Blue buses and ordered to sit quietly or face the consequences. All of the windows were open on these beasts which were not air-conditioned. After just a couple of minutes, we were all drenched in our own perspiration. I got a new appreciation for my nickname Butch on the bus ride from the airport to Lackland Air Force Base. During the bus ride, we were referred to as maggots, mamma's boys, ladies and my personal favorite dipshits. All of these made Butch sound like a pretty cool name. There were eighty of us on the bus. The majority were either from Pittsburgh or Philadelphia.

When we arrived at the base, we were assigned to 3701 Training Flight and were herded to our barracks. As a group (Flight), we were referred to as **PEOPLE.** The drill instructors made it sound like a dirty word. I came to really hate the sound of that word and the manner in which it was delivered. Once in the barracks, we were referred to as "Rainbows", because we were all in civilian attire that was made up of many colors. For the remainder of that day, we were herded from one place or another by Sergeant Story or one of his henchmen. Some of what we were going through reminded me of some of the movies I had seen. I marveled at the accuracy of the film industry. By day's end, no one complained about lights out coming at eight o'clock in the evening on a Saturday night. We were exhausted and some of us had not slept in almost two days. I remember lying in my bunk and hearing guys crying, cursing, praying and wishing they were back home where strangers did not call them really ugly names.

By Monday morning, we were getting to know one another and were starting to develop friendships. I sort of buddied up with a guy named Abbott who was also from the north side of Pittsburgh and a guy from Charleston, South Carolina by the name of Charles D. White. Charlie had flaming red hair, but because of his last name he was called "Whitey". The next "Curve ball" from God was delivered to the whole flight that Monday morning. We were fitted (Ha! Ha!)

for our uniforms and taken to the barber shop for our G.I. haircuts. When we came out of the barber shop, we all looked the same and bald-headed. No one could remember the names of anyone.   This confusion would last for several days until we received our name tags. I still remember standing in line in the barber shop laughing like crazy as hair cascaded to the floor. It took about two minutes for the whole haircut process. The only good thing about the haircut was that it only cost a quarter at that time. I pay nearly ten dollars for a haircut now at a local reserve base. My, how things have changed.

Our fatigues were at least four to five inches too long when they were issued. We were ordered to tailor them by reveille the next morning. God bless Gran Kimmel, for she had taught all of us to cook, clean, sew and fix things while we were growing up. That night was one of the funniest I have ever witnessed. We were all sitting on our foot lockers trying to get our fatigues to the proper length. I heard a lot of really bad language that night as guys stabbed themselves with needles or because they couldn't thread the needle. I had all of mine done in no time and was able to help Abbott and Whitey with theirs. The next morning was a riot, as we had guys showing up in fatigues that were either too long or too short or one leg shorter than the other. We were required to take all of our good dress uniforms to the base tailor shop, so that they would look sharp.

Basic Training was eight weeks of physical and mental training designed to make men out of us. We would go out to the parade ground at 0500. Five o'clock for normal people, however, what normal person gets up that early for exercise before chow. Chow is a military term for food, but there were a lot of times we could not identify what we were eating. I remember one morning, I was late to formation on the parade ground and was nailed by Sergeant Story. He shouted, "MAGGOT, WHY WERE YOU LATE FOR MY FORMATION this bright sunny morning?"

It was still dark for crying out loud. I made a GIGANTIC mistake by telling Sergeant Story that I was dreaming that I was driving my car and couldn't find a place to park. He took away my driver's license and kept it until the day we graduated from Basic Training. He threatened to have me arrested for driving without a license if it happened again.

On August 26, 1959, my birthday, we were given a partial pay and marched to the Base Exchange to purchase items from a list that was given to us by Sergeant Story.

There were several flights ahead of us and we were ordered to stand at attention until it would be our turn to enter the Exchange. Attention meant back straight, eyes forward, heels together with toes pointed out at a 45 degree angle, and hands at our sides with the thumb of each hand parallel with the seams in our trousers. My next "Curve Ball" came as I had allowed my left hand to relax to the point that my thumb was not along the seam of my trousers. Sergeant Story punched my hand so hard that the veins swelled immediately and the pain shot all the way up to my shoulder. Man, could that guy punch!

This "Curve Ball" was worse than having to share my birthday with my brother. It definitely taught me a lesson I would never forget. I always have my thumbs on my seams when saluting the flag or any other time when I am at attention.

When I enlisted in the Air Force, my recruiter assured me that I would be going to Air Traffic Controller Training and would become a controller. My next "Curve ball" from God came in week five of our training. We were marched to a building called "The Green Monster", because it was big and green. It was the building that housed personnel and career guidance. When my turn came to see the counselor, I knew exactly what he had in store for me: Air Traffic Control School. He hit me with the following statement: "After reviewing your records, test scores and assessing the "Needs of the Air Force" we can assign you to either Basic Medical Training or Air Photography School.

I said, "There must be some mistake, because my recruiter had me all set for Air Traffic Control School."

I don't think that the funniest comedian in the world could have gotten a bigger laugh than I did for my comments. The counselor acted as though I had just told him the best joke he had ever heard. At that point, I told the counselor that he could put me in for whatever he wanted.   At that point, I was so disappointed that I really didn't care where they sent me.

Once again, the magic forces in my life did it again for me and I was selected for Basic Medical Training at Lackland Air Force Base. As it turned out, I spent over 26 years in the medical field loving every minute of it. It seems as though the Air Force knows what it is doing when it comes to placing people where they are best suited. I will always have a profound respect for that system and be thankful for the opportunity I had to serve my country in that capacity.

The Armed Forces of the United States stole my identity at Lackland Air Force Base. I entered that installation as George W. Kimmel and left there as "Kimmel G.W., AF 13646398, AFSC 90230". In eight short weeks, the Air Force transformed me into this other person who was recognizable by numbers and anachronisms. The AF136646398 was my Air Force

Serial Number and the AFSC 90230 would be my Air Force job specialty.   A.F.S.C. stands for Air Force Specialty Code, as every job in the Air Force has a number attached to it.   The Army uses M.O.S. which stands for Military Occupational Specialty. We should have been allowed to pass through Basic Training just for memorizing all of this confusing and useless information.

My next "Curve Ball" from God came two days before graduation in the form of what would turn out to be my AFSC and next duty station.   As I stated earlier, my recruiter had promised me Air Traffic Control Training, but the counselor had ruled that option out.   In my disappointment, I had told the counselor to put me in for anything he wanted. Sergeant Story called all of us into the Squad Bay (a big empty room) for a special announcement. He had our orders for the various tech. schools we would be attending and we were about to learn our fate. He did this alphabetically, so I had to wait a little while to learn what the Air Force had in store for me. I was really getting excited as some of my "Comrades in Arms" were being read by Sergeant Story.

My fellow trainees, soon to be graduates, were heading for bases and places all over the United States. I was on pins and needles as I waited to hear where I would be going and what I would be doing to defend and protect my country. When your name was called, you were required to say "Here Sergeant", and Sergeant Story would bark out your assignment and then give you your travel orders.   I finally heard "Kimmel G. W.", and "Monkey" responded with my finest, "Here Sergeant."

I was told that I would be assigned to Basic Medical Training at Lackland Air Force Base. I was destined to take an exotic bus ride on the Air Force

Blue non-air conditioned bus across the base to my new billet. I found it hard to believe, but on my next payday the Air Force paid me fifty-four cents in travel pay from one barracks to the other. Just enough for a movie, popcorn and four cents in my bank account. Man, was I ever living it up now? To help heal my disappointment, God and the Air Force gave me my very first promotion.   I was promoted from Basic Airman (zero stripes) to Airman Third Class (one stripe). I got to put these new insignia of rank on all of my uniforms. I had survived and successfully made it through the eight weeks of Air Force Basic Training.

Flight Graduation Picture

Chapter 7
Basic Medical Training

My bus ride from the 3701 Basic Training Squadron to the orderly room took me all of eight minutes. This place was a mad house and for the life of me, I couldn't find anything orderly about it. After signing in, I was assigned Personnel Awaiting Technical School (P.A.T.S.) barracks to wait to begin my medical training. I had come from an almost sterile environment in Basic Training to the base's biggest garbage dump. People were constantly transiting through these barracks. No one was responsible for their cleanliness and it really showed.

They took the first guy to arrive and made them the barracks' chief. He got to wear a red rope on his left shoulder and boss people around. I understood that in some of the P.A.T.S. barracks that they had little versions of Hitler who allowed this small bit of authority go to their heads. I worried that I might fall into one of these barracks. With all of the disappointment I had gone through already, I just didn't need that on my plate at this stage of my young Air Force career. The guiding forces in my life stepped in once again and delivered Jay Thompson from Bangor, Maine as our barracks' chief. Jay was a great guy. He, Whitey (who was also selected for Basic Med) and I became the very best of friends. We didn't know it at the time, but we would be together for a very long time in faraway places. That will come later.

While we were in P.A.T.S., we were sent to a "Man Power Pool" and were directed to various locations on the base to do scut work. This included cutting grass, painting rocks and stones, commissary work and any other REALLY MENIAL thing that they could come up with.

The most dreaded of these duties was kitchen patrol (K.P.). It was the worst thing that could befall you. There were some guys who would pay someone to pull their K.P. for them, that's how bad it was. My first assignment to K.P. came on the start of our second week in P.A.T.S. When I saw "Kimmel, G.W." on the K.P. duty roster, I wanted to "Go Over the Hill" rather than pull it. My K.P. guardian angel would be in the form of Mess Sergeant Moore and I will always remember him as the guy who saved me from dish-pan hands or worse. When we reported to the Mess Hall for duty, we were all prepared for the worst day of our young lives. Mess Sergeant Moore took one look at my skinny, puny self and immediately assigned me to "Cook Shack" duty. My only job, on the dreaded K.P. was to have the cooks sign for anything they needed in the way of food preparation equipment. I was the man in charge of pots and pans. Man, was it ever an easy job. I guess it paid to be little and puny like Mickey Rooney rather than big and bad like Alan Ladd when it came to K.P. duty. Mess Sergeant Moore kept sending food out for me to eat. He said that he was trying to fatten me up a little. After two weeks of doing things a trained chimpanzee could easily do, we finally started Basic Medical Training.

Jay, Whitey and I formed a study group on the first day. We all did very well in Basic Medical Training. We even dissected a cat together as a team. I hope that my cat, Bacon, doesn't read this part of my book. It was during our Basic Medical Training that I met and came to know my very first Medal of Honor recipient. Staff Sergeant Washington taught anatomy and physiology. He was the very best Field Medic I have ever met. He won his Medal of Honor (Valor Above and Beyond the Call) in Korea, by saving the lives of several wounded men who were under enemy fire with great risk to himself.

He told us that the medical career field had more Medal of Honor winners than any other occupation in all branches of the military. He instilled a pride in all of us that stayed with all of us throughout our military careers. All of our instructors were extremely knowledgeable and were dedicated and loved what they were doing.

Basic Medical Training was eight weeks long just like Basic Training. It seemed to me that the Air Force seemed to think that everything that a person needed to know about any subject could be covered in that length of time. Some of the people in our Basic Medical Training class would go directly to work in hospitals and clinics upon graduation from Basic Medical School. Others would go to different bases for advanced medical training.

During Basic Medical Training, we were restricted to the base for the entire eight weeks. We were able to go to movies on the weekends and do some relaxing, but it was all done on the base. We got our first pass, off base, after our second week of Basic Medical Training. I was finally going to see some of the sights of San Antonio, Texas. We would be on pass from noon on Saturday (1200 hours) until six pm on Sunday (1800 hours). Whitey, Jay and I got all spiffed up and caught the bus into town. It was a great day. After being confined to the base for so long, it was really neat to see real people in regular clothes doing normal things. A number of our classmates were set on visiting the Alamo and the San Antonio Zoo. I would do both, but first I was headed to the nearest Woolworth's Five & Dime for a soda.

Back then, Woolworth's and stores like it, had soda fountains where you could just sit and enjoy a cold drink. As it turned out, there was a Woolworth's just around the corner from the Alamo. Jay, Whitey and I went there before we did anything else. It was the best and coldest drink I ever had.

I only visited San Antonio one other time while I was stationed at Lackland. I did not make a lot of money as an Airman Third Class and found things were a little more expensive downtown than they were on the base. I even made a little extra money by pulling barracks guard duty for those guys who wanted to go into town on the weekends. So, it worked out well for me in that respect.

My next "Curve Ball" from God came on one of those occasions. I was pulling a 0001 to 0400 (midnight to four am) on a Saturday night into Sunday morning shift. During that particular shift, we were not required to call the barracks to attention when someone of rank entered. All we had to do was make certain that the person signed the entry log, so that there would be a written record of all people coming and going. Chief Master Sergeant Robert D. Schultz (the Medical Squadron First Sergeant), whom we all knew by sight, came into the barracks at 0230 hours. He looked around, signed the log and left. He was really efficient and I saw no reason to challenge him nor to check his signature. Big mistake on my part. Chief Schultz called my name at reveille the next morning and asked if I had anything to report from my tour of duty as barracks guard. I stood at rigid attention and barked out, "No First Sergeant" as the proper response. Schultz shouted back, "Are you going to keep Mickey Mouse's visit to the barracks all to yourself or are you going to share the experience with your bunkmates?"

I had no idea what he was talking about until he SHOVED the entry log up my nose. There in big, bold print was the signature of Mickey Mouse in the time slot in which Chief Schultz had visited the barracks the night before. Everyone in formation had a side-busting laugh at my expense and I ended up with two extra tours of barracks guard duty as punishment. After that experience, I stopped pulling that duty to earn extra money. I would see and work with Chief Schultz again. We became really good and close friends. He did, however, tell the Mickey Mouse story every chance he got.

Basic Medical Training was just what the term implied. It taught us what we would need to know to function in a military hospital or clinic environment. Some of my classmates would be directly assigned to either a hospital or clinic upon completion of Basic Medical Training. They would then go through a period of on the job training in order to gain proficiency. A lot of these men would serve as Field Medics during the Viet Nam War.

Jay, Whitey and I studied very hard and worked together on all experiments. We even used each other's arms while learning how to give injections and draw blood (OUCH). Our instructors lied to us when they had us practice on oranges, stating that the orange had the same feel as the human skin. No way Jose!   When the human skin is **RIGID WITH FRIGHT**, it is much tougher than the orange as we found out (OUCH). Jay Whitey and I managed not to hurt one another enough to damage our friendship, but I do think that we all applied a little revenge when it was our turn to wield the needle. I really became quite proficient in the art of sticking needles in people and later would have patients request me by name.

By December, we were ready to graduate and learn our fate.

I know that I have said this before, but I will say it once again. The good Lord had his eye on me, Jay and Whitey and we were all assigned to Advanced Medical Training at Gunter Air Force Base in Montgomery, Alabama. We would first take a Delay in Route (leave) of 20 days before reporting in at Gunter. This would put us all home for the Christmas holiday. After graduation, Jay, Whitey and I made plans for when we would arrive at Gunter and said our "so-longs". We never said, "Good-bye."

Chapter 8
My First Air Force Leave

I really liked flying by now, but decided to take the Greyhound as it was a whole lot cheaper. What I didn't realize was that the Greyhound made frequent stops and that it would take me a day and a half to get home. Remember this was December of 1959 and I was in my winter wool uniform No civilian clothes were allowed even for travel. By the time I arrived in Pittsburgh, I really smelled like I had been on a bus for a long time. My mom and dad were at the Greyhound station to pick me up. I thought my dad was going to make me ride in the trunk. My mom (Ellen) wouldn't even give me a hug or kiss until I went home and cleaned up from my journey. Fortunately for me, Eddie was in school and by the time I would see her, I would not reek of travel by bus. This would be the first of many trips I would make by Greyhound, but those stories will come later.

One of the very first things I wanted to do was to get into old my civilian clothes and just relax and be normal while I was on leave. My mom thought that I looked spectacular in my "Blues" and wanted me to wear them instead of my Levi's and t-shirt. Gran and Pop McNemry were coming over for dinner on my first night home and my mom wanted to show me off to her parents. I have always been somewhat of a joker, so I dawned my Bermuda shorts, combat boots, dress blue shirt and a cap. I looked like I was set to go out into the desert and dig up dino bones. My mom was mortified. Pop McNemry laughed so hard that I think he may have wet himself a bit and Gran McNemry loved on me so hard I almost wet myself. My mom fixed all my favorites for dinner that night. I realized just how very much I had missed that part of my life while I was away.

After dinner, I put on my very best pair of Levi's, a new white t-shirt and headed off to see Eddie. What was it with the women in my life with the manner in which I dressed? Eddie was expecting to see me in my uniform and give me a hero's welcome home. We did have a great leave, but time flew by a lot quicker than any of us wanted it to.

Eddie was a senior at Saint Peters Catholic School for Girls and they were having a Winter Wonderland Dance during the time I was home on leave. My next "Curve Ball" from God came on the day of the Winter Wonderland Dance. While I was away, defending my country from "All Enemies Foreign and Domestic", my OVERSIZED brother Jim had helped himself to my wardrobe. He completely destroyed my brand new high school graduation suit. On the night of the dance, I discovered that the back end of the suit trousers was air conditioned as were both armpits of the suit jacket. It was too late to take it to a tailor, so I was forced to go to the dance in uniform. Thanks Jim. God stepped in, as he always has for me. Eddie and I were selected as the "King and Queen" of the dance. The D.J. spent the evening addressing me as "General" and even dedicated a few songs to us. As I look back on that evening, I realize that it was one of the best that Eddie and I would enjoy throughout our relationship.

My leave ended on New Year's Eve and it was time to say good-bye to everyone. Eddie and I had gone to a party at my Uncle Lou's and then back to my house to see my folks. I remember shaking hands with my dad, hugging my mom and kissing and crying with Eddie as we said good-bye at the Greyhound Station.

I remember looking out the window and already missing them all so very much.

We had no idea, at that time, when we might see one another again. I left Pittsburgh at one thirty in the morning on January 1, 1960. My next "Curve Ball" from God came during that bus ride. I was really tired from all of the New Year's Eve partying and I don't think that we were even out of the city limits of Pittsburgh before I fell big time fast asleep. While I was sleeping, the bus driver announced that he was having mechanical problems with our bus and that we would be changing to another bus in Wheeling, West Virginia. I totally missed all of this during my very deep slumber.

When we arrived in Wheeling, I got off the bus and went inside the terminal to answer nature's call. When I returned to Gate 3, our bus was gone and so were my bags with all of my uniforms, orders and everything I owned and would need to check in at my new duty station. I hit the panic button and went inside the terminal to find out about the bus. Our bus driver was just finishing his coffee and was about to call "All Aboard" for Montgomery. It turned out that the bus repair area was a three block walk and that I would have to get there, retrieve my belongings and get back to the terminal in fifteen minutes. That night, the good Lord literally put wings on my feet. I was able to make it there and back in time to catch my bus.

I stayed awake for the remainder of the trip and was really tired by the time we reached Montgomery. I got a room at a bed and breakfast near the bus terminal that night and went directly to bed. The next morning, I reported to Gunter Air Force Base for Advanced Medical Training. I would be there for the next three months.

Chapter 9
Gunter Air Force Base

This is a picture of the building I would be in for the next few months. As I look at this picture, I remember how many times I had to cut the grass while on a detail.

Gunter Air Force Base Annex is attached to Maxwell Air Force Base and both are located near Montgomery, Alabama. Alabama was a strange place for someone from Pittsburgh, Pennsylvania to be stationed at that time in our nation's history. Being from the north eastern part of the United States, I had absolutely no idea about the racial problems that they were having in the Deep South at that time. I remember how awe struck I was when I saw my first "Colored" and "Whites" separate drinking fountains and restrooms.

My next "Curve Ball" from God came as a result of these racial tensions during my second week in Montgomery and would be cause for us to be restricted to the base for nearly all of our time at Gunter. The entire twelve weeks. Like always, this restriction turned out to be a blessing for me, Jay and Whitey. We learned during the first week of school that all permanent assignments, after training at Gunter, would be based on class standing, so we studied very hard to stay near the top of our class academically. This would really pay off for us when we finished our training, but that will come later in this chapter.

We once again had some really great instructors in Advanced Medical Training. They prepared us well for the next phase of our careers. In addition to classroom studies, we received hands on training at the hospital at Maxwell Air Force Base Hospital. We did rotations through OB/GYN (Yuck), medical wards, surgical wards, clinics, and in orthopedics to give us some idea of where we might be assigned and what we might be doing when we reached our permanent duty stations. Jay and I were sold on trying to get assigned to a medical ward and Whitey had his heart set on working with surgical patients. We would all start out in our desired spots. We were also issued our first "hospital white" uniforms. Man, did we ever look like we belonged in a hospital. Except for looking like I was twelve, I really looked great in my Ben Casey's. Ben Casey was a TV doctor who was the big rage at the time.

My next "Curve Ball" from God was really funny (HA! HA! Funny, not ironic funny) and I still tell this story often. On the second Saturday at Gunter, Jay, Whitey and I decided to go off base for breakfast to a little place just outside the main gate. Our waitress was this very large blonde lady who talked really funny. She had the ultimate in southern accent. I ordered ham, eggs and toast, as they were my favorites at the time. When "Amazon Woman" brought me my meal, it had ham, eggs, toast and this mound of what looked like white sand. I made the gigantic mistake of asking the waitress what was on my plate. She put her hands on her hips, a snarl on her face and said, "Thems grits Yankee and you better eat 'em."

In fear for my life, I ate them before I touched anything else on my plate. The good Lord touched my taste buds that morning and the grits were not all that bad when I added a shaker full of salt and pepper and a pound of butter. I like to say that I ate grits twice on that day and refer to it as my first and last time.

Between classroom time, hospital time and study time, our stay at Gunter went by quickly and painlessly. Jay, Whitey and I tried our best to keep our academic records as close to one another as possible, so we could be certain to get our choices when assignment time arrived. When we graduated from Advanced Medical Training, Jay was number three in the class, I was number five and Whitey was number fourteen in a class of 40. Jay and I were reasonably certain that we would be able to be assigned together, but were a little concerned that Whitey might not make the cut.

Three days prior to graduation, the available assignments were posted on the bulletin board along with our class standings. There were only two locations that were posting three vacancies and we decided that we wanted to go to Fairbanks, Alaska rather than Frankfurt, Germany.

We did some inquiries among our classmates. Jay and I were assured our slots due to our class standing, but there was an obstacle to Whitey getting the third slot. There was a guy by the name of Gimbroni from New York City who was set on taking the third slot for Alaska. He was ranked 12th in the class standing. Jay and I went to work on him to change his mind. We offered him everything, but the kitchen sink. We could not budge him on his decision. We offered to pull duties, money and the naming of our future children to get him to allow Whitey to have the final spot to Fairbanks. The three of us had been through a lot together, and it appeared that it would be ending at Gunter Air Force Base in Montgomery, Alabama. Well at least Whitey was from the south.

How does the "Power" know when to step in and lend that helping hand? I have no idea how these things happen, but the USO sponsored a graduation dance and social for us on the night before we were to make our selections and Dino Gimbroni met and fell in love with a local girl by the name of Gert. He decided to take one of the assignments at Maxwell Air Force Base right there in Montgomery. The last I heard was that she and Dino married and had a slew of little Gimbroni's. The powers that be had once again stepped in and saved the day. Jay, Whitey and I said our "so-longs", and made plans to meet in Seattle for our military flight to Alaska. We would, once again, have a 30 day "Delay in Route" before reporting to McCord Air Force Base for our flight. It seemed like all I did that first nine months was go home for visits.

I drove north to Chicago with one of our other classmates when we departed Gunter on the Thursday a week before Good Friday of 1960. Through letters, I had made arrangements to visit with my mother, her husband Don and her two children Gary and Shirley for a few days before going home to Pittsburgh.

I had a great visit with my mom and her family. I was happy for the life she had found with Don and the children. Don was really good to my mom and the children were a joy to be around.

Remember the names Gary and Shirley, as they will be the cause for one of the funniest "Curve Balls" in my life. Gary talked me out of an Air Force hat, belt and some of my chevrons that he insisted my mom sew on one of his t-shirts right away. He wore that shirt the remainder of the time I was there. Don, my mom and their family showed me a great three days in and around Chicago. I was more than a little mad when the time came to leave. We all cried a little, promised to write and to get back together again just as soon as we could. We did write the whole time I was in Fairbanks.

I even got letters from Gary and Shirley. Gary absolutely loved the military and would one day graduate from The United States Military Academy at West Point.

I took the "Red Eye" train from Gary, Indiana to Pittsburgh, and really enjoyed my very first train ride. My next "Curve Ball" from God came during that train ride in the form of a little old lady I did not know and would never see again. I had two pieces of luggage with me on the train, and one of these made the little old lady from nowhere quite angry. One of my pieces was a B-4 bag. It was a combination garment bag and saddlebags for accessories. When folded for carrying, it had a flat, fake leather, center upon which I had attached a bumper sticker I had purchased on my car trip to Chicago. The sticker read, "Of all my relations, I like sex the best" in big bold print. I hadn't noticed during the train trip, but every so often, the little old lady from Cleveland was glancing across the aisle and reading my sticker.

When she got off the train in Cleveland she gave me the dirtiest of looks, a smack on the shoulder and said, "You G. I's are all alike, just one thing on your mind."

When I got home, my mom gave me the same look and a similar comment. She told me that I would have to remove that sticker before she would allow that bag in her house. No more baggage tags for me after that.

I arrived home on Good Friday of 1960 and would be home for a little over two weeks. You know this Air Force life wasn't all that bad, as I had been home for Christmas, New Years and now Easter in just my first nine months of service. Good Friday has also been my favorite holiday since way back in 1955.

To make a little extra money and take up time during the day, I worked for my Uncle Lou while I was home on leave. I was really surprised at how much I remembered about meat cutting and did really well at it during that leave. It was also good to see some of the old customers and of course telling them about my new life with the Air Force. I also did the restaurant deliveries for my Uncle Lou and got to meet Johnny Unitas during one of those deliveries. He was having breakfast at one of the restaurants when I was making a delivery and the owner introduced me to him. It was really cool to meet the great "Johnny U" as he was known back then. He was a local boy from Pittsburgh.

This leave was a lot like before I entered the Air Force. I worked during the day and spent my evenings with Eddie. We did a lot in that two weeks and the time flew by quickly. Eddie's brother Jack came home one weekend while I was home. It was great seeing him again. Once again, Eddie and I promised to write each other and did well for a while in keeping those promises. What most people don't understand is that military life is just like civilian life, but it's done in a uniform. It can be pretty routine and downright dull at times.

People think that there are exciting things happening all the time and that a G.I. should have tons of things to write about. Letter writing would become a major issue during my time in Alaska. It would also bring some heartbreak. Due to the fact that I was going so far away and would be gone for a long time, I made the effort to go by and see as many of the aunts, uncles, cousins and grandparents as I could during that leave. I also visited with as much of Eddie's family as I could. I reasoned that it would be a very long time before I would see and visit with them again.

Chapter 10
North to Alaska

My journey to Fairbanks would begin at McCord Air Force Base in Tacoma, Washington. I was really beginning to like all of this traveling and I think that it was becoming habit forming. Even today, my feet start to itch once I have been in a place for two or more years. Whitey was the first to arrive and he made arrangements for rooms for Jay and I for when we arrived. We had room on either side of Whitey and it was good seeing them again. Whitey had a "Curve Ball" of his own on the night before Jay and I arrived when he lost over one hundred dollars in a "Floating Poker Game". We were cautioned about getting into these kinds of games during transit, but "Old Whitey" was one of those guys who had to learn the hard and expensive way. We were only in the transit barracks for one day and night and then on a plane bound for Alaska. We flew on an Alaskan Airlines military charter flight and made a short stop in Anchorage before going on to Fairbanks. Even back then (May 1960), the Anchorage air terminal was quite impressive. They had stuffed bears, caribou and moose everywhere. They had a giant Kodiak bear that was shot and killed by a woman using a handgun. That had to be one tough and nervy lady.

We arrived in Fairbanks in the middle of a beautiful May afternoon. I received a minor "Curve Ball" when I got my first view of Fairbanks, Alaska on that warm spring day. It was 70 degrees for crying out loud. I had this image in my mind of snow, igloos and Eskimos. I was deeply disappointed by the sight of this modern looking city with people dressed normally.

Downtown Fairbanks in 1960

It had been a long time, but I once again found myself on an Air Force Blue bus from the terminal to the hospital squadron. Jay, Whitey and I were all in awe of the summertime sights of Ladd Air Force Base.

This was the sign at the main gate.

I think that the realization of just where we were really hit us when we saw and read this sign for the first time. In time, this sign would be cause for our bragging rights about how far north we really were. Ladd Air Force would later become Fort Wainwright, so I would guess that pictures are all that remain of the old main gate sign.

The next "Curve Ball" from above was delivered to me, Jay and Whitey when we signed in at the hospital squadron. We learned that all of the rooms in the barracks were two man rooms and that the three of us would all have roommates who were already assigned to rooms. We were all hoping that we would be assigned to the same room, but that was not to be.

Once again, those forces that have always looked after me, stepped in and saved the day. My new roommate turned out to be a really great guy by the name of Dick Charest. He would play a major role in my Air Force career. Dick was married and had a baby daughter back in the "Lower 48". That was Alaskan terminology for the continental United States. He was also a sports parachutist and a really great medic.

I would go out and watch Dick jump out of air planes and help him gather in his chute after he landed. I don't know how many jumps he made, but he was really good at it. He landed on target well over 90% of the time. He had me so fired up about skydiving that I wrote my dad asking him to sign the enclosed parental permission slip, as I was under the age of 21. My next "Curve Ball" from above was my father's letter of response. I waited for what seemed like forever for a letter from my dad. About three weeks later, it finally arrived. The letter simply said:

> Dearest Son,
> Not just plain no, but **hell** no!
>
> Love,
> Dad

In another letter which I received from my mom (Ellen), she explained that my dad loved me far too much to allow me to do something that dangerous. I still went out and watched Dick jump, but it was somehow not the same after my dad's denial. I am probably lucky that my dad said no back then. I think he said no, in part, for all of the accidents that my brother Jim had while we lived on Osgood Street. Parents have a tendency to be protective like that. It would take me a few years, but I would end up in my father's shoes.

Dick also ran a one man clinic at the hospital. He did all of the EKG's (heart tests), pulmonary tests and assisted Dr. Bowers in surgical clinic on Wednesdays and Fridays. He worked straight days (Monday through Fridays) with weekends and holidays off. What a set up! Dick was due to rotate back to the United States in December and asked me if I would like to train for his position. WOW!! What a great opportunity this would be for me. There go those special forces working their magic for me once again.

I trained hard and when Dick rotated to Altus Air Force Base in Oklahoma, I was appointed the new EKG technician. I stayed in this position for the remainder of my time in Alaska.

Jay worked on the medical ward and volunteered for straight nights. At first Whitey and I were baffled. Jay would later transfer to the medical clinic and would be on straight days like me. Jay fell for and ended up marrying the night nurse he worked with on the ward (mystery solved). He is the only one of my Air Force friends who has been married longer than me. He married in 1961 and Barbara and I would not tie the knot until June of 1963.

Whitey got his wish and ended up working on the surgical ward for the whole time we were stationed in Fairbanks. He got so wrapped up in it, that he planned to go to medical school when he got out of the Air Force. He loved wearing the green surgical scrubs and went out of his way to get blood on them. He would also rather be caught dead than be caught without a stethoscope around his neck. He turned out to be a really good surgical technician from what I gathered from some of the nurses and doctors that he worked with. I lost track of Whitey after we left

Alaska and can only wonder if he did go to medical school. I hope that he did and that he has had a great career.

My next two "Curve Balls" from above came through the mail or the lack thereof. The first was from Eddie. She wanted to know if I would have a problem if she took a date to some of her school functions. I realized that I really had no control over that situation and I reluctantly said that it would be alright. Little did I know, at the time, but she was already dating a guy when she sent me that letter. It wasn't long after that time when her letters became fewer and fewer and farther apart. The frequency would pick back up when I was getting ready to rotate back to the United States.

It worked out for both of us, as I dated a couple of different girls while I was stationed in Alaska. The second mail "Curve Ball" came as a result of me not writing home as often as my parents thought I should have been. I remember coming in from work and finding a note taped to my door telling me to report to Captain McLaughlin the next morning at 0800. Captain McLaughlin was our squadron commander, a really fair guy and someone we were all proud to serve under. I had NEVER been summoned to any Commanding Officer's office and was a nervous Wreck by the time 0800 rolled around. I reported in and the captain had me sit in a chair opposite his desk. Remember, that I was still little and puny and looked really young, so this guy and this situation really scared me. The captain opened our conversation with, "How often do you write home to let your parents know how you are doing?"

The question caught me a little off guard and I said, "Sir, as often as I can."

Little did I know, but my dad had called him the

day before and told him that he had not heard from me in over a month. The captain ORDERED me to sit outside his office right then and there and write a letter to my parents. He said to make certain to apologize to them for not writing sooner. When I was finished, he read the letter and ordered me to mail it that day. He also ordered me to bring him my letter home every Friday for his review to make certain that I was following his orders. I know that my folks got more letters from me than I got from them after that.

Football was really big in Alaska at the time and Ladd AFB had several other military teams that they played against. The games were played at one of the base fields every Saturday afternoon. We were fans of the Ladd Air Force Base team and we cheered them on to victory every chance we got. I had also become friends with one of the star players. His name was (IS) Ferdinand Gonzalez, but everyone called him Speedy.

Speedy also worked at the base theatre and would sneak us into the movies through a side door. What a guy! At the time, he dated an Army Major's daughter by the name of Nancy McCoy. We would all become good friends and Nancy and I went out to the movies together after Speedy left Alaska.

One Saturday afternoon, Speedy was injured on the field of play and was admitted to the hospital where I worked. I went to see him the first thing Monday morning. I picked up his chart and read that he had a hematoma of the calf. This was fancy medical jargon for a bruise. In a nervous voice, Speedy asked me what a hematoma of the calf was. I told him that it was really bad and that we would probably need to amputate the leg. Speedy and I are still great friends today and still talk about that day and all we did while we were stationed in Alaska.

Christmas Day of 1960 was the loneliest day I had ever spent up to that point in my life. I worked a shift on the medical ward from 0700 to 1500, (7 To 3), went to Christmas dinner in the mess hall and then dragged myself back to my room. When I opened my door, the radio was playing "Blue Christmas" by Elvis. I am a HUGE Elvis Fan, but I still cannot hear that song without thinking of that Christmas. I plopped down on my bed and was really feeling sorry for myself. Just then there was a knock on my door and the CQ told me I had a call from home. Hello, guardian angel.

By now, you should be able to tell that I am a man of faith who believes that there is a "Guiding Force" in one's life that is greater than themself. I think that this faith was strengthened by some of the examples of the handiwork of God that surrounded me in Alaska. One of the most beautiful examples of this handiwork was revealed to me during the winter of 1960 and 1961.

We had a two week period when the outside temperature stayed at -45 degrees or lower and the whole base was covered in snow. It was so cold that the moisture in the air froze and crystallized. At night, the lights from the moon, street lights and passing cars would reflect on the crystals and make them appear as millions of tiny stars dancing in the air. There were nights when I endured the extreme cold just to watch this magnificent example at the hand of our maker. Even the Northern Lights could not compare with this show. By the way, you could also breathe the cleanest air on the planet in Alaska.

During the summer of 1961, the Air Force would turn over Ladd Air Force Base to the Army and they would re-name it Fort Wainwright. As Air Force personnel rotated out, they were replaced by Army troops. I had the honor of being one of the last members of the Air Force stationed at Ladd AFB.

When Dick Charest departed, I got a new roommate by the name of Norman Anderson. Andy, as we called him and I would be roommates for the remainder of my time at Ladd. Andy was from West Virginia and was and is one of the nicest, kindest and gentlest men I have ever known.

We had some really great times (basketball games, all night poker games and all night bowling) over the time I had remaining in Alaska. Fortunately, you have not heard the last about Andy, as we will meet again down the line and are even in touch with one another today.

Mail was one of the most important parts of our lives up in the frozen north and I was really blessed with my fair share almost daily. I received mail and care packages from Beverly Hines, my folks and best of all from my Aunt Roma. My Aunt Roma has always and still does make the very best ever peanut butter cookies. They were so good that the guys would even eat the popcorn she packed them in because they said the flavor of the cookies was embedded in it.

Our mail clerk, a guy by the name of Lou Rice, would tell the whole barracks when I received packages with my Aunt Roma's address on them and there would be a line at my door when I got back to the barracks. I still, to this day, alert my Aunt Roma when I am going to be in Pittsburgh. She makes it a point to have some fresh baked cookies just for me. My wife has a goal to one day make them as good as my Aunt Roma.

One day in October of 1961, Whitey asked me if I would go with him to the home of one of his surgical patients. It seems that Dr. Bowers had agreed to allow this patient to go home, provided he had someone to change his dressings daily and keep an eye on the surgical site for signs of infection. Whitey volunteered, but got cold feet when the time came. I went with him and it turned out to be one of the best and smartest things I had done in a while. The patient's name was Joe Kerokos and he and his family turned out to be some of the nicest people I would ever know. Mrs. Kerokos was a cook on par with Gran Kimmel. The aromas coming from her kitchen reminded me of home. She made, from scratch, the very best enchiladas I have ever tasted to this very day.

I started dating their oldest daughter shortly after our initial visit and would be her steady for the remainder of my time in Alaska. Her name was Barbara and she was a really sweet girl. I just couldn't seem to shake the name Barbara. Barbara and her family were devout Catholics and I started going to mass with them every Sunday. I made up my mind that I would become Catholic when I returned to the states. Eddie was Catholic and we had started corresponding once again. I will always remember the Kerokos family and Barbara. I count myself fortunate to have known them.

In November of 1961, just six or seven weeks before I was due to rotate back to the states, the Air Force made an AFSC designation for EKG/Pulmonary Function Technicians. At that moment, I became a 91650 Cardio-Pulmonary Technician. All Air Force personnel who had been performing these duties were automatically given this new designation along with promotions. I was going home an Airman Second Class. I realized that I would always owe a great debt to Dick Charest for getting me into this new and exciting career field, and for the major role it would play in my future. Due to the nature of the work, I would always be assigned to a major medical facility, either stateside or overseas. This would be critical to my personal life once I married and started a family of my own.

In December of 1961, Jay, Whitey and I would depart Alaska for our new assignments. I was headed for Sheppard AFB in Wichita Falls, Texas. Jay was going to a small base in Maine not far from home. Whitey was going to Charleston AFB in his hometown. Jay and Whitey were really going home and would finish their Air Force careers in their respective hometowns. Jay was going home with a new bride and was really excited about his family meeting her. I never saw Jay again after we said our so-longs at the Seattle airport. I often wonder how his life turned out. I hope he reads this book and contacts me some day.

Whitey decided to visit my family in Pittsburgh before heading to Charleston. He and I traveled by bus from Seattle to Pittsburgh and the trip took over three days. It was a great trip, as the bus was filled with G.I.'s and college students heading home for the holidays. We partied really hard on that trip and it turned out to be the best bus ride I ever took. We did, however, really reek when the bus pulled into Pittsburgh. Both Whitey and I had to ride in the back seat of my dad's car with the windows rolled down.

Whitey spent three days at my house and I showed him all the sights of Pittsburgh. He was fascinated by how close some of the old houses were in some of the old neighborhoods and by the Crafton Incline. Due to the fact that they both had red hair, I think that Whitey developed a little crush on Eddie during his stay with me. I put Whitey on a bus at the terminal five days before Christmas and, like Jay, I never saw him again.

Eddie and I became engaged on Christmas Eve of

1961. Both our families seemed happy that we had reached that stage in our relationship. I popped the question in my dad's car in our favorite parking spot in Riverview Park. I asked, she said yes and the flashing lights went off. It seems that the city of Pittsburgh had a rule that there was no parking in the park after dark and the flashing lights were from a police car. When I explained the circumstances to the officer, he said, "Kiss her one more time and be on your way".

Eddie and I went to her house to break the news to her family. Her brother Jack was also home on leave and he had gotten engaged to a girl named Cathy just two days earlier. The Dailey family was about to marry off two of their children in the very near future, or so it seemed.

I had a really great leave and, like always, it ended far too soon. I don't know how this keeps happening, but on my last night home we went to a New Year's Eve party at my Uncle Lou's. After the party, we went by Eddie's house so that I could say my good-byes to her family. We ended up at my house, and my folks, along with Eddie, drove me to the Greyhound station. We said our good-byes and, little did I know at that time, but I would never see Eddie again (curve ball).

Whitey Shooting Craps

Andy Shooting Craps

Chapter 11
Everything's Bigger in Texas

I arrived at Sheppard AFB on January 2nd of 1962. This would turn out to be what I would later refer to as "The Turning Point in My Life Assignment". I remember taking a taxi from the bus terminal to the base and the cab driver telling me that all base personnel were restricted to the base because of a big fight between the locals and the airmen on New Year's Eve. I was not in uniform at the time, so I just sort of blended in. We would always travel to town in groups of three or more due to the continuing problem with the locals.

This new assignment would introduce me to some new friends and people who would become important to my life and future. My new roommate was a guy named Randy Markley who was a personnel specialist with the hospital squadron. He also did auto repairs at night and on the weekends to earn a little extra money. He will really mess me up later. Our next-door neighbors were Gary Sanders and Gus Mylak. We lived in an old WWII style barracks that had been converted into two-man rooms.

This was long before the 1,000 man dorms that the Air Force has today. Gary Sanders and I would become close friends and he would play a very important part in my future.

Eddie and I wrote each almost daily and were saving money for our future. I had sent her money while I was in Alaska and during the time I was at Sheppard. She was even planning a visit to me in June of that year (1962). My next "Curve Ball" from above changed all those plans and would culminate in the termination of our engagement and my future with Eddie. In March, I received an urgent call from my dad. He was calling to see if I had any money that he could borrow.

It seems that my brother Jim and two of his friends decided to go to California, but had little money and **NO** transportation.   The police caught them somewhere in Ohio, after they had stolen their fourth car. My parents, along with the other parents, were responsible to pay for all damages and towing of these cars. I contacted Eddie and told her to give my dad all of the money I had sent her. This was about $800. She went nuts on me and said that my dad could find his money somewhere else and that I didn't care about her or our future. My dad had always been there for me and there was no way or no one who could stop me from helping him. She told me that if I gave the money to my dad that we would be ancient history. I told her to give my dad the money and the engagement ring that very day. My dad got the money, sold the ring and was able to clear up the mess that Jim had made. I never heard from Eddie again. I would see her brother Jack one more time, but we never discussed what happened between me and his sister. I understand that she married a couple years later and had two or three sons.

When my dad paid me back a couple months later, I bought a 1956 jet black Buick Special convertible. It was, as I said, jet black and had a red leather interior. I paid $750.00 for it. I saw one like it the other day on line and they were asking $25,000.00 for it. This car and Gary Sanders would introduce me to the girl I would marry. Gary was dating Barbara Piatek in the spring of 1962 and would introduce us at one of his baseball games. Gary, like Barbara, was an only

child. Gary's over protective mother didn't think that
Barbara was the girl for him and they did not last very
long. Regardless of Gary's mom, their relationship
was doomed from the moment I set eyes on her. As I
said, Gary played baseball on the squadron team. He
would ask me to sit with Barbara so that no other
guys would hit on her. Little did he know that this
was a gigantic error on his part. Barbara had the
most beautiful long and shiny hair, the biggest brown
eyes and a smile that was to die for. I had more than
a crush on her. I am a firm believer in love at first
sight, since I am the victim of such a circumstance.

Barbara was the babysitter for MSGT Bob
Cornelius. The Cornelius's lived just across the street
from Barbara and her parents. One day after work,
Bob asked me for a ride home and insisted that I put
the top down. I drove Bob home in my shiny black
convertible. Barbara and the Cornelius girls were
playing in the front yard when I dropped him off.
After I dropped him off, he and Barbara had a little
discussion about her knowing me from the time that
she dated Gary. Bob told me the next day that I
should call Barbara and ask her out on a date. This
was late May of 1962. I called her the next day to
ask. She said she would go out with me. We made a
date for the next Friday night and I was on pins and
needles waiting for Friday to arrive. I will never forget
how absolutely beautiful she looked when I picked her
up. She wore a beige colored silky looking dress and
looked stunning in it. We went to the Wichita Theatre
and saw the Elvis movie "Follow That Dream". How
appropriate, I never dated another girl after that
night. Barbara lived at home with her parents and her
father was really strict with her. He scared the 'ELL
out of me. He allowed her to go out on a date one
week night and either Friday or Saturday on the

weekend. I was allowed to call her in between our dates. Her phone number was 723-2820 back then and I called it so much that I never forgot it. He did allow her to attend my confirmation classes once a week and didn't count them as a date. Barb's mom was great from the start. She and I would become as close as I was with Gran Kimmel and my mom. She was always after Barb's dad to treat me nicer than he did. He and I would become the very best of friends. I loved and respected him as much as I did my own father. We have a picture of them that hangs in every house we have ever owned. Every once in a while, I still ask them for advice.

My next "Curve Ball" from above nearly ended my relationship with Barbara. I had asked her out on a Friday night. She had declined for some reason that I can't even remember now. After chow, I decided to visit the home of my boss.   Frank and Millie Highlander were two of the nicest people on earth. I babysat for them and went to their house all the time. Frank even let me borrow his car before I bought mine. At their house, I was allowed to just walk right in. On this particular Friday when I walked right in, there sat Barbara with several of my friends including Gary.   I immediately turned and left.   I was determined that I would break off all ties with the girl who didn't have time for me that Friday night. I drove around for a while, went to the Airman's Club for a beer and then back to the barracks. Gary, Davie Yost, Andy and some of the other guys were waiting for me when I got there. They told me that Barbara and the Highlander's were planning a surprise 21st birthday party for me on the following Sunday. They made me swear to act surprised and not to tell Barbara that they had told me about the surprise. It was a success and I acted surprised. Barbara has never thrown me another surprise party if that tells you something.

Barbara and I became engaged on Thanksgiving day in 1962. Her mom sent us to the Mini Mart to get something and I popped the question in my car in front of the store. When we got back to the house, Barbara showed her ring to her mom and Terri Elliot. The Elliot's were Barb's mom and dad's best friends who had come over for Thanksgiving dinner.   I remember Barb's mom saying, "You better go tell your dad."

I remember how frightened we both were. Her dad just looked at us and said, "We will talk about this later."

The rest of the day was very long and uncomfortable for us as we waited for the talk we knew was coming. The Elliot's left at about 7 pm and Barbara and I prepared ourselves for the **TALK**. Barb's dad said that he knew that this day would come. He asked us if we knew what we were doing and just when we planned to tie the knot. He talked us out of the first three dates we had picked and we all finally settled on June 22, 1963.

Barbara and I did a lot between Thanksgiving and June. By the time we got married, we were pretty well set up. Barbara worked in the warehouse of the Base Exchange. She saw and picked over all of the new merchandise as it arrived.   She bought flatware, silverware, linens and all sorts of getting started items. I think that by the time payday rolled around, she owed most of her pay back to the Exchange. Barbara's folks bought us a beautiful bedroom set. Fifty years later, we still have and use it. We use it in one of our guest rooms and it looks as good as the day we got it. Thanks mom and dad. I called Barbara's folks Mom and Dad the minute we got married. They always made me feel like the man they would have chosen for their only daughter.

My next "Curve Ball" from above came during the planning of the wedding. I had never told Barbara that my parents were divorced. I didn't know how to tell her that I wanted to invite my dad, stepmother, my mom and my mom's family.

Barbara has always been able to read me like a book and she knew that something was bothering me about the wedding plans. When I explained it to her and her folks, they acted like it was no big deal and told me to invite them all. Barb and I sent out the invitations. We got a really great response. I would have both sets of parents, my grandparents Kimmel, my brother Bob and my mom's children Gary and Shirley. Barbara would have half of the Polish population of East Chicago and Hammond. Both cities are in Indiana. We were going to be married in chapel two on the base by Chaplain Father John Ulrich Lee. Father Lee was a great priest. He really knew how to put people at ease. He answered his office phone by saying "Chapel two, Pope John, how may I help you?"

I kept telling him that word was going to reach the Vatican and that the real Pope John was going to call him one day.

Three days before the wedding, Barbara's family arrived from up north. All I could see when I drove her home from work were either Illinois or Indiana plates. I tried just dropping her off, but she insisted that I come in the house and meet them all. As soon as we walked in, the conversation switched from English to Polish. I didn't have a clue what these people were talking about, but I did hear the word George every so often. I knew that I was being scrutinized by the clan, but felt a little helpless at that point. I finally spoke up and said, "I know that you are talking about me, but I wish you would do it in

English so that I might defend myself."

That statement broke the ice and we all became instant, lifelong friends. I became as close to some of Barbara's family as I was to my own. That's what family is all about.

My family arrived next and stayed at the rental house that Barbara and I would live in after we got married. Barbara and I met them on the little bridge that separates Texas from Oklahoma just outside of Burkburnett, Texas.

It was great having all of them there for this most important day in my life. My dad fell in love with Barbara the minute he laid eyes on her. He told me to be good to her and to take care of her. He and I had a couple of father and son talks over the next two days. He was really happy that I had found Barbara. He had always told me, "Son, find the woman you want to be the mother of your children and marry her before someone else does."

He felt and knew that Barbara was the one. My mother, Don, Gary and Shirley arrived later that day. They stayed at the Cardinal Inn just outside the main gate to the base.

Counting family from out of town, our friends and our co-workers, we had over 100 people attend the wedding. I will always remember Barbara and her dad coming down the aisle. She was, and still is, the most beautiful woman inside and out that I have ever known. I remember saying to Dino, my best man, "Man, look at her, I am the luckiest man alive."

She was breathtaking! Our wedding was combined with a mass that was said mostly in Latin and I am still a little uncertain about when, in the ceremony, I actually became a married man. I knew it was a done deal when Father John said, "Ladies and gentlemen, allow me to introduce for the very first time anywhere,

Mr. and Mrs. George W. Kimmel." He then instructed me that I should and could kiss the bride.

Barbara and I on Our Wedding Day

Barbara's mom and dad hosted a big party at their home that evening. There were people everywhere and all seemed like they were having a great time. It was a really great party that stretched into the next day. The party goers wore out the living room carpet that night. My new Polish family certainly knew how to have a good time. Barbara and I formed a reception line and were able to greet and thank all of the fine people who helped celebrate this very special day. I didn't know it at the time, but our wedding pictures would be some of the last pictures taken of my Grandmother Kimmel. A "Curve Ball" to come later. My new bride stayed in her wedding dress for the party, but I changed into my baby blue dinner jacket. Barbara would change into a dress when we got ready to leave the party later that evening. While the party was going on, my brother, my mom, Barb's mom and Barb's cousin Stormy would empty Barbara's suitcase. When we arrived at the motel, Barbara excused herself and went into the bathroom. I heard a loud scream and turned around to see Barbara holding an empty suitcase. The only thing the culprits had left in the bag was her hat for church the next morning. After a few frantic phone calls, we were able to convince my brother and Stormy to bring Barbara's things to the motel. We stayed in Wichita Falls that night so that we would be around to say our good-byes to both families who were leaving on Sunday, June 23, 1963.

After church the next morning, Barbara and I drove out to our house in Burkburnett to say good-bye to my family. This would be the very last time I would see and hold my Gran Kimmel. We had breakfast at the house with the family and then they left for Pittsburgh. I felt really blessed to have had them all there for the best day of my life. My brother Bob would enlist in the Army shortly after they got home and he would come to visit us later. I missed my brother Jim, but he and the two other boys from the California adventure were in a teen detention facility at the time.

Next, we drove over to Barbara's folk's house to say our good-bye's to Barbara's relatives. There were some of them who were still partying. Of which, a couple who looked like they had been hit by a truck. Barbara's folks looked tired, but I think that they were happy that this was coming to an end. I think it was Ben Franklin who said, "Fish and visitors smell after three days."

I think that her folks wanted to air out the house and settle back down. We said our good-bye's, thanked them all for coming and promised that we would visit them as soon as we could.

Barbara and I had planned to stay in town until Monday morning before leaving on our honeymoon. We had planned to go to this brand new amusement park in Arlington, called Six Flags over Texas. Yes, this is the very same park that exists today. It opened the year before Barbara and I wed. We had planned to drive there and back in our not too reliable 1957 Ford. I felt certain that it would make it there and back, but was a little leery.

When we went to say our good-bye's to my mom, Don, Gary and Shirley, Don suggested that we go to Six Flags in their car, as they were also planning to go there. Don said that he would buy us bus tickets back to Wichita Falls. We decided that we would take Don up on his generous offer. We started out bright and early the next morning for Arlington. Don had a brand new Olds 98 so was it ever a nice and pleasant ride to Six Flags. We stopped in Bowie, Texas and had a great breakfast, which Don paid for. As it turned out,

Don paid for almost everything on that trip. I think that he knew that Barbara and I didn't have a lot of money at the time.

Six Flags was great. We did everything there was to do that day. Barbara and I really liked the traveling singing groups they had back then. Gary and Shirley did all of the little kid things and Barbara and I sort of paired up with them on most of the rides. How great was this? Butch had taken his mother and her family on his HONEYMOON. I know it doesn't sound very romantic, but we really did have a great time. We stayed at Six Flags all day and were really tired when we left the park. Gary and Shirley both fell asleep on the tram on the way to the car and then again in the car from the park to the motel.

We had not made any reservations and were not certain we would find a place that late in the day. My next "Curve Ball" from above came when Don signed us in at the Six Flags' Holiday Inn. Don went in while the rest of us stayed in the car. When Don came out he was grinning from ear to ear. He was able to get us a suite so Barbara and I would have one room and Don, Mom, Gary and Shirley the other. Don paid for the motel as he had for our tickets to Six Flags. The problem with the suite was that my mom and Don could open and enter our room, but we could not do the same from our room. Don has always been a guy who loves to **TEASE**. He teased Barbara and me almost all night long. He would shout, "I know what you two are doing and I am coming over there."

I could hear my mom telling him to stop, but I think that she was enjoying it too. We had a great stay at the Six Flags Holiday Inn. Don and my mom were lucky enough to meet another couple during our stay that they became lifelong friends with. I still get teased every once in a while about taking my mom and her family on our romantic honeymoon.

Six Flags Holiday Inn
June 24, 1963

Barbara at the door to our room...

My
mom by
the
pool...

   The next morning, Don and family drove us to the Greyhound Bus Terminal. They put us on the bus for Wichita Falls.   I really enjoyed being with Don, my mom and children. We really did have a great honeymoon.   At least it was one we could talk about for a long, long time. We arrived in Wichita Falls that afternoon to begin our new life as husband and wife. We stopped off and had dinner with Barbara's mom and dad and then went to spend our very first night in our first home. We would only live in the little house in Burk for a couple of months before we would move into base housing. The house in Burk was small, but I will always have a fondness for the very first place we called home. Sadly, I couldn't find a photo of that little house to include.

My birthday is August 26th and Barbara's is August the 20th. We were given an early birthday present when we were selected for a one bedroom duplex on Childress Street on the base. It was a great little place and only two blocks from Barbara's mom and dad. The nice thing about base housing was that the base paid for everything except your phone bill. Texas was super-hot in August, so I kept my thermostat on a minus number.

I can still see the neighbors looking at Barb's mom when she came to visit us. She always had a heavy winter coat draped over her arm and would put it on before entering the "Freezing Zone" I called home. Barb's mom and dad did not have a lot back then, but she never came to the house empty handed. She kept me supplied with root beer popsicles all summer long. The four of us spent a lot of time together and Barb's folks made me really feel welcomed as a member of the family. It was great having family around again for Thanksgiving, Christmas, Easter and all of the other important days. On our first anniversary, Barbara prepared a gourmet meal of hot dogs and beans served on our never-before-used china by candlelight. Mom and dad came over with a card, money and a box of popsicles.

My next "Curve Ball" from above was delivered on January 11, 1964. I will always remember it as one of the saddest and darkest days of my life. It was a Friday night and Barbara and I were at the Twin Falls drive-in movies. All of a sudden our names appeared on the screen telling us to come home immediately. Remember, there were no cell phones back then. Mom and Dad were waiting for us when we arrived at the house. I still remember mom telling me that Gran Kimmel had passed away. No one knew it at the time, but Gran had cancer and was in a lot of pain when she came to our wedding. I know that I would never want her to hurt at all, but at that moment I was so happy that she had been at our wedding. I still have the deepest of love for Gran, even today. Barbara and I left that night bound for Pittsburgh to pay our last respects to the woman who had raised me. We drove from Wichita Falls to Hammond, Indiana on the first leg of the journey. We stayed with Aunt Jo and Uncle Paul who had attended our wedding. Barbara was big-time car sick for most of the trip to Indiana and I was really happy to stop. We arrived in Pittsburgh on Sunday morning. Gran was going to be buried on Monday. Pop Kimmel asked me, Bob, Ralph, Ronnie and two other cousins to be pall bearers.

I would have the honor of carrying "Mum" to her final resting place. Remember how those "Guiding Forces" in my life were always stepping in to make my "Curve Balls" tolerable? Well, it turned out that Barbara was not suffering from car sickness, but from morning sickness. We were going to have a baby. The "Powers That Be" were going to send me someone to help fill the hole left in my heart by Gran Kimmel's death. Our daughter, Karla Lea Kimmel was born at 4:09 in the afternoon on August 19, 1964. She was sent to help fill a void. She was so lovely and perfect that she did the job. I know that Gran Kimmel was looking down to make certain that I was healing alright and I know that she loves Karla from afar.

Mom: Giving Karla
Her First Bath

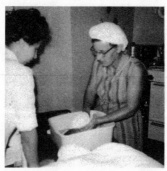

We had given up our house on base, and moved in with mom and dad. They had a nice three bedroom house in a little town called Iowa Park. By then, I had orders to go back to Alaska, and mom and dad thought that we could save a little money by living with them. It was the best and smartest thing we ever did, as mom was a great help with the new baby. The Air Force had a strict rule back then about how old a baby must be before it could fly on an Air Force plane. I was on orders for September to go to Elmendorf AFB in Anchorage, but Karla could not travel on an Air Force plane until she would be three months old. Leaving Barbara and Karla behind was one of the most difficult things I have ever had to do. I was devastated the day I left for Seattle.

Chapter 12
Way Up North

I arrived in Anchorage in September of 1964 and would not see Barbara and Karla until late November. They were in good hands with mom and dad. I knew that they would be alright. I set about getting settled in and getting accustomed to the Alaskan winter. It snows in Alaska in late September. Then, you don't see the ground again until spring. It is also dark about 20 hours a day. It can be a very depressing place. I was fortunate to have some old friends from Sheppard there to help me adjust.

My new boss at Elmendorf was a guy I knew from Sheppard, so the transition was an easy one. Jerry Blakeman was the craziest son of a gun I have ever met in my life, but one of the nicest people God put on this earth. When he received his orders for Alaska, he FAKED a heart attack to try to get out of the assignment. They put him in an ICU Unit and he fell in love with and married his night nurse. Shirley was the right woman for Jerry, as she had the patience of a saint. They have a daughter who is close to the same age as ours. Jerry kept me in the dog house with Barbara all the time, but Barbara loved him like the big brother she never had. Jerry was just so nice that people could not help but like him. The night before Barbara arrived, Jerry took me out to celebrate, and man, did we get plowed. We went in my car and Jerry got really sick all over the passenger side. It was very cold in November in Alaska and his mess froze to the side of the car to include the door handle. The first sight Barbara had of Anchorage was Jerry's vomit all over the side of my car. Without missing a beat she said, "I see you and Jerry were out on the town last night." I told you the woman could read me like a book.

Our first house in Alaska was in a sub-division called New Naka Valley, but Jerry called it "No Nookie Valley". It was a cozy little one bedroom only ten minutes from the hospital. There was no natural gas in this house and we did everything with the use of propane. The one thing you did not want to do was run out of propane, so we checked the meter daily. We did run out one day and Barbara carried Karla to a friend's house over two blocks away. It was cold and snowy, but she did it. We didn't have a lot back then, but we did enjoy the people I worked with.

We always (almost seven days a week) had someone at the house. John Vaughan, who was recently divorced, came over a lot and taught Karla how to crawl and then walk. A guy we all called Chili Bean came over as well as Jerry and the Goodson family. We played cards to all hours of the night, went bowling in the middle of the night and really had fun with all our friends. We were all far from home and our real families so this seemed to draw us all very close.

You know that Alaska is known for its beautiful sled dogs (Huskies). Well, Chili Bean worked at the base vet's office and he gave me my next "Curve Ball", in the form of a Husky puppy. This dog was absolutely beautiful, and had the eyes and markings of a good Husky. The problem was that he was dumb as a brick, but I came to love him in spite of it. I named him Gomer Pyle after the TV character of the same name. Gomer followed Karla everywhere and the two of them got into everything. When it was time to leave Alaska, they wanted more money for Gomer to fly than it would cost me for Karla. Who knew they could charge so much for a dog? It was a sad fact, but it looked like Gomer would live out the rest of his life in Alaska. It's ironic how some things work for the best in all our lives. Shortly before we were to leave Alaska, Barbara sent me to the Mini Mart for bread or something and Gomer rode there with me. Gomer stayed in the car, but when I came out there was a Major standing by my car talking to the dog. He said that Gomer was a beautiful animal and asked where I had gotten him. Gomer went home with the Major right from the Mini Mart that very afternoon. I felt good that he would have a good home and that the Major would have a great pet.

Gomer begging like always!

I must have really been happy to see Barbara when she finally arrived in Alaska, as she became pregnant soon after her arrival. Kari Lynn Kimmel would be born on June 22, 1966. Barbara really got the hang of making babies and gave me the two most beautiful girls a guy could ever ask for. By our calculations, Barbara would become pregnant on New Year's Eve of 1966, and give birth to our first son nine months later. I blamed it on the fact that we did not have HBO back then and on the fact that I ate a lot of chunky peanut butter.

We lived in two different base houses during our tour in Alaska. The first was a four-family apartment complex on the main street of the base at Elmendorf. We even had to share the washers and dryers and had certain days when we could do laundry. That was the toughest part with Karla still in diapers and Kari coming along. The walls were so thin that we could hear our downstairs neighbors argue every single night. This place was also across from the main runway and the hanger where they repaired jet engines. We could hear them revving up jets almost every night.

It was nicer than New Naka Valley and we had really nice neighbors. Our neighbor, Jim, from downstairs got me a part- time job in a gambling hall. I worked at that job until we left Alaska and it paid for a lot of nice things for all of us. It was a fun job. Barbara would come out on Saturday nights to play Bingo. We would all go bar hopping when our club closed and we had a ball. Chili Bean would take care of the baby and later both babies. I took my very naive wife to her first strip club and she got the opportunity to meet "Miss 48". The 48 did not represent her age or IQ. We also went out one night while Barbara was very pregnant with our second daughter. I went to the restroom and while I was gone some young airman from the base came over to ask Barbara to dance. When I came back to the table, she was laughing like crazy about what had happened. She said that when she said yes and stood up that the guy took off like a scared rabbit after his apologies. We had all really healthy babies and Barbara was quite large during all her pregnancies.

In 1966, the Army at Fort Richardson, started deploying troops in large numbers to Viet Nam. They opened up some of their really nice housing to Air Force personnel. Fort Richardson and Elmendorf were joined by a common road and I was actually closer to work when we moved there. The Army gave us a great house that had a basement plus a lot more room than our Air Force housing. We lived there for the remainder of our time in Alaska. I was still working Monday through Friday with all weekends and holidays off and we had the time and money to see and do a lot in Alaska. Karla learned how to ice skate on a pond near the hospital. I would take her skating almost daily. The only problem I had was she would not want to go home and I froze my butt off.

We left Alaska on June 29, 1967. Barbara was over six months pregnant with our third child at the time. We decided to drive to our next duty assignment which was in Florida.

Barbara's mom came to Alaska and would drive back with us to help with Karla and Kari. The Air Force and the Canadian government placed very rigid requirements for driving the Alcan (The Alaska Highway) and we had to make a lot of modifications to our Rambler station wagon. Before we started on our journey, I asked Dr. Finney, "What do I do if Barbara goes into labor?"

He said, "Just boil water." This was that what they

had done in every movie he had ever seen. He said that Barbara would probably be a little uncomfortable, but that she should make the trip just fine. It took almost four days to navigate the Alcan. It was a long and dusty trip over a very rough road. We could only drive at speeds of 35 to 40 miles an hour due to the condition of the highway. We had an amusing "Curve Ball" during this trip that we still tease Kari about. Kari was absolutely hooked on the pacifier and was impossible without it. We took four or five with us when we left, but after the second day we could only find two. Mom watched Kari and as she grew tired of the pacifier she would throw it out the window. Stops were few and far between and it took us about four hours to reach our next one. They only had two pacifiers in stock and we bought them both. Mom tied them to a ribbon and pinned them to Kari's shirt each day. Those two lasted us until we reached the states. God, was I happy that mom was with us on the trip. We crossed over into the United States on the 4th of July, 1967. We crossed over in Great Falls, Montana, but not before we encountered a "Curve Ball" from Barbara.

Our final city in Canada was Alberta and we came through during the Calgary Stampede. This was a really big celebration in Canada. The roads were not marked well and we had no GPS back then, so we got lost. Barbara spotted a car with Montana plates and said, "Follow that car." As it turned out, the car with the Montana plates led us to a really nice Canadian shopping mall. The people had come to Canada to do their weekly shopping, but were nice enough to give us good directions to the U.S. After that day, the whole family would tell Barbara to look for Montana plates anytime we were lost. It became, and still is, one of the family jokes that we use on one another.

Barbara has a great sense of humor and takes it all in stride.

We were able to complete the remainder of our trip without further incident. We drove to Aunt Jo and Uncle Paul's where we spent time visiting Barbara's family. I probably gained a few pounds on that trip as everywhere we went, we were expected to eat. Barbara had a great family and they all made you feel really at home.

The next leg of our journey took us to Pittsburgh to visit with my family.   Both my brothers were married by then and we got to meet their wives on this visit. Bob and his wife lived two doors down from my folks, so we saw a lot of them while we were there. It was great seeing the family and visiting with some old friends from school.

The final leg of the Alaskan adventure was our drive from Pittsburgh to Fort Walton Beach in Florida. It had taken us over three weeks of driving to reach our final destination, but it was a journey we would all talk about for years to come.

Chapter 13
Eglin AFB 1967 to 1969

Eglin would be my first and only assignment in the Sunshine State during my Air Force career. We would encounter a lot of "Firsts" with this assignment. We would buy our first house, get sued for the first time, buy our first and only mobile home and have our first son. Eglin AFB was near Fort Walton Beach and we would buy a house that was across the highway from the water. My cardio-pulmonary career would allow me to work my regular Monday through Friday schedule and give us ample opportunity to see and enjoy what Florida had to offer. Our dream is to one day retire in Florida.

Barbara's dad got a "Remote" assignment to Thailand and mom would stay with us for our first year at Eglin. It was great having her as she was great with the kids. She had been with us for the birth of all three of her grandchildren. She and Karla became really close during this time. They would take a drive every evening to the post office to mail letters to Barbara's dad. Mom and Barbara also had some time together. They would go shopping and to Bingo at the Knights of Columbus Hall. Mom also had some of her own friends who were stationed at Eglin. They were people she knew from her time in Germany. It worked out well for all.

The first house we tried to purchase was in a great area right on the waterfront. The owner allowed us to move in prior to closing and we started setting up home. One day, I stopped by the office to see how our loan application was progressing and was thrown a "Curve Ball". Our loan had not yet been submitted, and would not be submitted until we agreed in writing to pay off a couple of bills that we had at the time. None of this was in our original contract and I refused to do it. Moe Hirsh, the owner, said that we would have to move if we did not agree. I was really upset when I went to work the next morning. I had no idea what to do. Roy Boyle, who worked for me, saw that I was upset and asked what was wrong. When I told him of my predicament, he said that he saw a guy putting up a "For Sale by Owner" sign on his way to work. He said the house was just around the corner from where he lived and that it was in a great area. By the time I drove over to the house, there were two other guys already there. Due to the base, housing was always in demand. The two guys were haggling over the two hundred dollars equity that the owner was asking for. Yes, I said $200.00. So, I handed him $250.00 and sealed the deal. The total cost of the house was $15,000.00. What a buy! Welcome to Tuxedo Drive.

Two days later we moved into the first house that would have our names on the deed and mortgage. Moe Hirsh accused us of fraud when we attempted to purchase his property and he took us to court. He accused us of just staying in his house while we searched for another house. He was also trying to charge us for damages he claimed we made to his property. This guy had the biggest case of "Liar-Liar, Pants on Fire" that I had ever seen. On the day we went to court, I wore my Class A uniform with all my stripes and decorations on it. It paid off. The judge believed Barbara and me. He dismissed Moe's case on the spot.

The house on Tuxedo Drive was great. We lived in it almost until the time we left Florida. It was a three bedroom brick home that had a backyard the size of a football field. There was a swing set in the farthest corner of the yard. Kari would be completely naked by the time she reached it. The girl just hated clothes.

There was a family who lived next door that had five children. They had a boy named Michael who had Downs Syndrome. Their father was also on a remote tour in Thailand leaving the mom there with the kids. Michael soon became my constant weekend and after school companion. He would go everywhere with me. He would come over to our house right after school every day to see me to get cookies and milk from Barbara. His mom always knew where she could find him. He helped me cut the grass, take down the trash and wash my car. We would then drive to Dairy Queen for our pay. Michael was, however, a real handful for his mom. She could be seen chasing him down the street almost every day. She would have a cigarette hanging from her mouth, dragging a belt and shouting, "Michael, I'm going to kill you if I catch you."

One day Michael was running up the street and I decided to do my best impression of his mom. She caught me right in the middle of my act. She didn't speak to me for weeks. We still remained friends after and on Christmas Eve I assembled all of her children's Christmas gifts (bikes, wagons and doll carriages).

Paul Lewis Kimmel, my first born son, was born on September 29, 1967. Are you paying attention to how close apart my kids were born? I must have had a little of my dad in me. He was a really big baby and they kept him in Neo-Natal ICU for a couple of days. I had a son who I couldn't go near or hold. I bought him a small football and gave it to one of the nurses to put in his bassinette. The nurse in charge was a lady by the name of Captain Duckworth. She drove me crazy. She would pick him up and hold him in front of the nursery window. She said he looked like a sissy and wanted to know what to do with the football. Barbara said that after I left, Captain Duckworth would hold Paul and rock him back to sleep.

My dad and stepmom came to visit us in May of 1968. They stayed almost a whole week in a motel a few miles from the house. They would take Karla and Kari swimming at the motel every afternoon. Karla called it Papa's Motel long after they went back to Pittsburgh. My dad was complaining about a pain in his shoulder, so I took him out to the base to see one of the doctors I worked with. Dr. Myzell thought that my dad had a torn rotator cuff and advised him to have surgery when he got back home.

The worst "Curve Ball" that I had received, thus far, in my life did not prepare me for the Friday night phone call I received three weeks after my folks returned home. My mom was crying so hard that I could not understand what she was saying. She put my brother Bob on the phone. He told me that when they opened my dad up for the surgery that they found cancer everywhere in his body. I could not even remember the last time my dad had a cold, let alone something this drastic. They started him on chemotherapy, but to no avail. My dad died on August 31, 1969 at the young age of 48. I flew home right away. I did pretty well until I saw my dad in his casket. I have never cried so hard or have been so shaken up in my life as I was at that moment. There were still things I wanted to talk to him about and advice I knew I would need, but all of that was gone. I still talk to my dad. I feel certain that he hears me. There are still times when I miss him so much and would like to sit down with him, but they pass.

My next "Curve Ball" caused me to put a request in

for a new assignment. Back in the 60's and 70's when promotions came out, you were given what they called a line number to let you know when you could sew on your new stripes and the promotion became official.

One day my boss, Chief Pego, called me into his office and handed me a piece of paper with some numbers on it. He said it was my "Line Number" for promotion to Technical Sergeant. I was on cloud nine. I rushed home to tell Barbara the great news. On the day of the promotions, I was not called to the commander's office for congratulations and the customary set of new stripes. I then, went to see Chief Pego in his office. He said that he could not figure out why I had not been called and he made a call to base personnel. The look on his face after that call told it all. Would you believe that there were two George W. Kimmel's on the same base at the same time. Chief Pego had only gotten the names of the people who had been promoted and not their service numbers. The other George W. Kimmel was the one who had gotten the promotion. I was devastated. I dreaded having to go home and tell Barbara.

After the promotion fiasco, Chief Pego said that he would make some calls to see if he could help me get transferred back to Alaska. Barbara and I decided to buy a mobile home and have the Air Force ship it to Alaska. We would live in it while we were there and sell it for a big profit when we left. The best laid plans often go astray. Eleven days after we purchased the custom-made home, I received orders to go to Japan. We had purchased this home unfurnished, as we wanted to put in and use our own good furniture. Now we were going to have to find a buyer that wanted to do the same. My life's "Guiding Forces" stepped in once again and we found a buyer who gave us full price and on we moved.

The Air Force had a strict rule that members had to report to Japan, secure base housing and then the family could be shipped over. Barbara's mom and dad were stationed at Williams AFB in Arizona at the time. They insisted that Barbara and the kids stay with them while they waited. I told you before that they were great parents to us all. We loaded up the car, visited family in Pittsburgh and Indiana and then headed to Luke. I spent two weeks at Luke before I went to Japan and the folks really showed me a great time. Barbara and I spent as much time together as we possibly could, as we had no idea then how long we would be separated. After my stay in Arizona, I drove to Travis AFB in California. The Air Force would ship my car and I would fly out from Travis to Yakota.

On my journey to Japan, we made stops in Hawaii, Wake, Okinawa and Yakota, Japan. On the plane, I sat next to two young boys who were on their way to Japan to be with their Navy dad. These two little rascals beat me out of $12.00 playing poker on the plane.

Chapter 14
The Land of the Rising Sun

I landed at Yakota AFB in Japan on July 4, 1969. My home base and final destination in Japan was Tachikawa AFB which was about a forty minute bus ride from Yakota.   I went through Japanese Immigration and Customs with no problems, then headed outside to catch the bus to Tachikawa. I had never thought much about being in a foreign country until I got on that bus.   Every person on the bus, including the driver, was Japanese. The driver spoke a little English and assured me that I was on the correct bus.   Sure enough, we arrived at Tachakawa about an hour later. I was never so happy to get off a bus as was that one. It was hot, slow and filled with people speaking in a language I did not know or understand.   I would be in Japan for almost three years and learned very little Japanese. The Japanese speak very fast and in a sing–song-like tone.   It is difficult to learn the language by listening to people on the street or on the bus.

My new supervisor, Ron Pittman, met me at the bus stop in front of the hospital squadron.   He, his wife and two sons welcomed me and took me to their house for lunch. Over lunch, Ron gave me a briefing about some of the people and what I would be doing. Tachakawa Hospital was an old WWII ramp style hospital and they had cardio-pulmonary spread out over several locations within the hospital.   Since I would be the ranking Staff Sergeant, Ron was putting me in charge of the Pulmonary Lab which was right up my alley. Ron had not been in Japan very long, but it seemed as though he and his family really liked it.

After lunch, Ron took me back to the squadron orderly room and got me checked in. I was assigned to room with a guy I already knew from my assignment at Sheppard AFB. J.C. Watts and I worked together at Sheppard and it was really great to see a familiar face. J.C. and I would room together until Barbara arrived. He was a really nice guy. He made me a big George Jones fan. He had every record that George had made up to that time. Since it was a holiday, there wasn't much I could do but unpack and try to get squared away. I was really tired, but it was really too early in the day to go to sleep, so I unpacked, wrote a letter to Barbara and did a "recon" of my surroundings.

The hospital squadron occupied one whole corner of the base and was like its own little community. We had a movie theatre, exchange, chapel, barber shop and a small restaurant called the Civilian Club. I ate the biggest and best shrimp I have ever eaten at the Civilian Club. I went there a couple times a week while I was in bachelor status. They also had slot machines and pool and ping- pong tables, so it was a nice place to hang out. I hated being separated from Barbara and the kids and stayed on top of trying to get base housing.

I had Ron Hoey, Jimmy Spires and Chuck Davis under my direct supervision. Ron was from New York. Jim was from Ohio and Chuck was from Washington, D. C. They were all very knowledgeable and hard workers. They made my section the pride of the department. Ron lived in the barracks behind mine. Jim was married and lived in base housing and Chuck had a room in the barracks, but also rented a little house off base. We would all usually have lunch and dinner together in the mess hall and then go to a movie or two at one of the NCO Clubs.

Chuck Davis invited me over to his Japanese house on the second Friday I was in Japan. He said that he would like for me to see an authentic Japanese house and experience a meal served Japanese style. Chuck also invited his landlords, the Sanobe brothers. It was a great experience. I became very good friends with the Sanobe brothers. When I arrived, I took off my shoes at the door and put on some sort of sandals that Chuck handed me. We sat on the floor around a circular table and were served dinner by the Sanobe brothers' wives.

Chuck had warned me that it would be considered an insult to refuse anything that was offered and with that in mind I remember tasting things that I really don't like to talk about. I ate squid embryo, snails, raw fish, soybean Jell-O and some really funny looking crackers. I washed it all down with far too much Kirin Beer and Sake. I would pay the price for days to come. A good Sake hangover can last for days and give you a headache that is the mother of all headaches. My particular first time Sake hangover lasted until Tuesday of the following week. This included Saturday, Sunday, Monday and part of Tuesday. People around you recognize the symptoms, and avoid you at all costs.

Before coming to Japan, Chuck was stationed in Thailand, and became intrigued by the Buddhist Monks. He told me that the Monks had taught him how to read the cards and asked if he might read mine. You know that I do not believe in that sort of mumbo - jumbo, but I did not want to offend my host. Chuck read my cards and predicted a long life and many children. At that time, I was smoking almost three packs of cigarettes a day. The thought the long life prediction was a little crazy. I already had three children, so I figured that the many children part was right on. Barbara was not yet in Japan and Chuck has never met her. When Chuck turned over the next card, Chuck told me that Barbara was pregnant and that she was going to have more than one baby.

I was in Japan and Barbara was in Arizona at the time, so I really didn't see this prediction coming to pass. I just figured that old Chuck had just one Sake too many and the cards were a little blurred. One week later, I received a letter from Barbara telling me that all that time we had spent together before I left for Japan had ended in pregnancy. On March 8, 1970 our twins Ron and Robbie were born and fulfilled Chuck's last prediction. I am still not a believer in mumbo - jumbo, but there may be something to this Monk card reading.

A very pregnant Barbara and the children arrived at Yakota Air Base in November and we were able to begin our new life in the Land of the Rising Sun. Paul was just a little over two years old at the time and hated wearing shoes. He came off the plane in his stocking feet and ran directly to me when he spotted me in the crowd. He ran right under the barrier that separated the arriving passengers from those of us who were waiting. Deciding that Paul was not a threat to Japanese Security, the Japanese immigration inspector said that Paul could stay with me and that he would expedite the rest of the family. He kept his word to me and in short order, I was surrounded by the women in my life. I was never so happy to see anyone as I was then.

Ron Pittman and family, Ron Hoey, Chuck and the Spires family were all there to meet my gang and to help with all the baggage. We drove from Yakota to our temporary quarters in a giant complex called Green Park. We would stay in Green Park for a week or so, before moving into our house on Grant Heights.

We got really lucky with our Grant Heights house, in that, the Pittman's lived just around the corner and our new next door neighbors had a girl Karla's age and a boy Paul's age. Al and Irene Gonzalez would become our very good and close friends.

All of the houses came furnished with furniture from the base. It was nice and the wives had some say in style, color and particular pieces. We were also allowed to ship several thousand pounds of household items at the government's expense. We shipped our dishes, pots and pans, linens, kids' toys and a small portable television set. The day our household goods arrived was like Christmas for the kids. Paul had been waiting for his bike and I didn't think that we were ever going to be able to get him off the darn thing. We had the movers put the portable TV in the girls' bedroom. I turned it on just to see if it still worked and it played just fine. About an hour later, Karla came running down the stairs all excited to tell us that Gilligan already knew how to speak Japanese. We all got a laugh out of that and still tease Karla about it.

At that time, there were American programs on the Japanese stations, but all of the dialog was in Japanese. It was a riot to watch programs like "The Lone Ranger" and hear both The Lone Ranger and Tonto speaking Japanese. The kids watched Japanese cartoons every Saturday morning and swore that they knew exactly what they were all about.

Barbara went into labor with the twins on Saturday March 7, 1970. And they were born the next day just a few minutes apart. Both mom and babies were fine and our family size had just increased by two. We now had five children and the oldest was just five and one half. Due to the instant increase in our family's size, the Air Force moved us into a really big house on the main street of Grant Heights. We were just across the street from the movie theatre, exchange, commissary, dispensary and the headquarters building. The base flag pole was directly across the street from the house and my three oldest went out every morning and evening to watch the parade. This is what they called raising and lowering the flag every day. They all stood at attention and saluted as the flag went up and down the pole.

While Barbara was in the hospital making twin babies, I was at home playing Mr. Mom. I do not envy any woman and mother on the planet. Motherhood would drive me crazy if I had to do it on a permanent basis. I had a really cool system worked out for meal times during the time Barbara was in the hospital. We had cereal for breakfast and I only had to throw four cereal bowls into the dishwasher. We had marshmallows and Cokes for lunch, served on paper products. We went to the NCO Club for dinner and Paul and Kari ate for free. I only had to pay for me and Karla and she really didn't eat a whole lot. It was a great system and all were happy with it. One day I left the children with Irene Gonzalez, so Barbara and I could have a little us time. By the time I arrived at the hospital, Barbara was ready to have me strung up for child abuse. It seemed that my loving children did not want to eat the really healthy soup and sandwiches prepared by Irene, but opted for their regular lunch of marshmallows and Cokes. It was a great system while it lasted, but we ate a lot healthier after the soup and sandwich incident at Irene's.

Due to the escalation of the war in Viet Nam, we were forced to work longer hours and to take on some very new responsibilities. Me, Ron Hoey, Jim Spires and Ron Pittman were all trained to work in the Hemo Dialysis Unit. When a person is severely wounded and they lose a lot of blood and body fluids, their kidneys shut down. We were getting these types of patients almost daily and I saw and assisted in the treatment of some really horrendous results from the battlefield. The majority of the patients we treated never made it back home due to the severity of their wounds. I gained a new appreciation for the Memorial Day holiday during the time I served in Japan. The average age of our patients was between 19 and 20, and it was a rough time for me both professionally and personally. It made me realize that war was a young man's endeavor.

Japan was really becoming industrialized by the time we arrived and the air pollution in and around Tokyo made Los Angeles seem like the cleanest city on earth. The locals all wore surgical masks everywhere they went to help them breathe. My next "Curve Ball" from above came when I found out that I developed what was called Tokyo/Yokohama Asthma due to the air pollution. There were nights when I sat up all night coughing and fighting just to breathe. By the winter of 1970, I was in and out of the hospital as a patient. Dr. Rosenbaum finally decided to air evacuate me from Japan due to the severity of my symptoms. All of my lab work (blood work, pulmonary tests etc.) were at very dangerously low levels and my prognosis for recovery was not good. On March 7, 1971, one day before the twins' first birthday, I was air evacuated to the hospital at Travis AFB in California. Barbara and all five kids followed on a commercial flight the next day. She has to be the toughest lady on the planet. She traveled with all five kids all by herself from Japan to California and the whole time she was worried about me. Barbara's folks met her at Travis the next day and drove her and the kids to their home in southern California. I was able to call Barbara every day, but it would be a while before I would see them all again.   My health improved daily after my arrival at Travis and I was feeling better and stronger all the time. All of my lab work was approaching normal. I was finally given a pass from the hospital. I bought a car when I became ambulatory and was able to get out and about. I went to see Barbara and the family just about every weekend while I waited to get my assignment to a new base. During the week, I worked in the cardio - pulmonary lab at Travis and I was happy when I finally received my orders assigning me there.   I immediately made arrangements for Barbara and the children to join me.

Chapter 15
California Here I Come

It was next to impossible to get base housing right away, so I went on a waiting list. After paying an outrageous deposit because we had five kids, we moved into a nice three bedroom house in Vacaville, California. This is the same city which houses federal inmates in an institution for the criminally insane. This was and is the place where Charles Manson, the *Helter Skelter* killer was being held. Barbara worried that he would escape and kill us all in our sleep. We did not live in Vacaville long before we were selected for a house on the base. We played hell getting our deposit back from the landlady as I remember.

It was really nice being in California and we went to visit with Barbara's folks every chance we got. I really got to know the highway system between the two houses really well. Barbara's folks also came north to visit with us. It was great being a family once again. The job I had at Travis was as the NCOIC (Non-Commissioned Officer in Charge) of the pulmonary lab and respiratory therapy and I did the same things I did in Japan. I was, once again, on a fixed shift Monday through Friday. I had all of my weekends and holidays off. Barbara's dad was really becoming big buddies with all three boys and they did everything together. They would also do just about anything dad told them to do. One morning we found the four of them at the table with bowls on their heads and oatmeal running down their faces.

I was grand-fathered into my line of work just before I left Fairbanks. The Air Force did not have any specific training for my career field at the time. The

Air Force would be forced to send their qualified airmen to the Navy school in San Diego. The Navy course included hands-on and academic training at the Naval hospital. It tied up an airman for a year. This was costly and timely. Due to all of this time and expense, the Air Force decided to develop its own program.

An announcement came out requesting volunteers from throughout the Air Force to establish this program. I had always admired and respected all of the trainers I had at all of the various schools I had attended, so I felt that this might be a good way to pay back my debt to the service. I would also get to pass on my experience to new people coming on board. Since I had only been assigned to Travis for one year, I didn't think that I stood much of a chance to be selected for this duty. Do you remember the statement that the counselor made to me at the Green Monster so long ago? "Due to your experience, test scores and the needs of the Air Force, you are qualified for Basic Medical Training or Air Photography?" Well, it appears that when the needs of the Air Force are involved, nothing else matters. I was selected over the phone in an interview with MSGT Joseph Nash who would be the new cardio-pulmonary program director. Joe and I would develop, write and teach in this program for nearly four years.

Chapter 16
The School of Health Care Sciences

The School of Health Care Sciences is located at Sheppard AFB near Wichita Falls, Texas. I felt like I was returning to the scene of the crime. The School of Health Care Sciences was where ALL Air Force medical training took place. It was fairly new and quite innovative. In addition to the new cardio-pulmonary program, it was also starting a new physician assistant program that would become well known throughout the medical field. The base and town had not changed in appearance, however, there had been a population explosion. There were a lot more people and businesses that had opened since my last tour of duty there. Today, it is like a ghost town as a lot of the training that was done at Sheppard has moved to other bases. A lot of the businesses have closed and there is not a lot of activity downtown.

I would be required to attend and successfully complete the Air Force Technical Instructor Course before I would be permitted to step into a classroom. I really owe a lot to this program, as it prepared me for some golden opportunities later in my life for both my career with the Air Force and beyond.

The course was designed to teach us the finer points of being a classroom and field instructor. I will always remember a sign that hung in the main entrance to the training building that read: "I Couldn't Even Spell ENSTRUCTER, And Now I Are One." Most of our instructors were civilians who had all been and still were classroom teachers. They showed no mercy when it came to having us do things the correct way. It was the toughest school I had attended up to that time, and we all called it the enema school. That meant high, hot and hell of a lot. There was no rank among the students or in the training and we were all treated the same. We had a couple of Captains from the Turkish Air Force, one Major from personnel, a couple of Lieutenants and the remainder of the class was made up of enlisted personnel. The class also represented just about every career field in the military. The training lasted eight weeks. We were required to give a speech or teach a class just about every day during that eight weeks. This class was NOT a walk in the park and we lost several guys who just could not cut it. I am really grateful to all of my prior mentors and friends who showed me how to stick with it. I received my first "Curve Ball" at T.I.C. on the second day of training. We were required to reach into a box and pull out a piece of paper with instructions written on it. We were then required to give a five minute presentation on what was written on the paper.

I drew a piece of paper and it instructed me to give a five minute formal presentation on the finer points of a button. I had learned that as an Air Force instructor, I was to do the following in all presentations:

1. Dazzle the students with your brilliance.
2. Baffle the students with your very best B.S.

I am happy to say that I used both techniques on my button presentation and was well on my way to becoming an Air Force Technical Instructor. I would attain the ranking of Master Instructor before my tour of duty ended.

In addition to teaching you classroom methods of instruction, the course focused on teaching us to be confident, how to dress and how to carry oneself in the classroom setting. I am happy and proud to say that I excelled in all areas. It was as if this was what I was meant to do. I reached a point in the training where I felt that I could and would do a good job teaching in T.I.C. I was flattered when a couple of my instructors made those types of comments on my graduation evaluation. I really liked and still like being a formal classroom instructor. I wore the uniform and the instructor insignia with a great deal of pride.

Instructors were also treated very well all over the base. There were special lines at the exchange, barber shop, gas station and commissary that were designated for "Instructors Only" which was pretty cool.

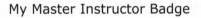

My Master Instructor Badge

We were still required to give two graded classes at our duty location when we completed T.I.C. Each class had to be 50 minutes in length, but could be on the subject of your choosing as long as it fit into the class schedule. I decided that I would teach my two classes in the new physician assistant program. I taught the classes how to do arterial punctures and how to read pulmonary function tests. Both classes went very well and I was cleared to teach.

After I graduated from T.I.C., Joe Nash and I would begin to write the course materials for the new cardio-pulmonary program. We spent all of our on and off duty time writing lesson plans, ordering text and reference books, ordering supplies and getting our classrooms ready. Our first class was due to report for training in late August. This first class would have seven students. It became known as the "Magnificent Seven". By early July, we were ready to receive and teach our classes.

I flew out to California to get Barbara and the family and to clear base housing at Travis. We had a Mercury station wagon that we loaded to the MAX. We cleared base housing and went to stay in a motel for the night. The kids were all small at the time. They were easily bored with the motel. That evening we went to a street carnival just to get the kids out of the room and to relax a little before we hit the road for Texas. My next "Curve Ball" from above was delivered at that carnival in the form of a goldfish that Paul named Otto. Paul won Otto the goldfish at one of the games of chance. He was determined to take Otto to Texas. Barbara went to a local store and bought a large bottle of mayonnaise, which would become Otto's new home for the journey to Texas. The next morning, we loaded luggage, the children, the dog and Otto into the old station wagon and headed off to our new home. The drive would take us two days. Paul wanted me to leave the car running every time we stopped so that Otto would not get too hot. I don't know how he did it, but Otto survived the drive.

We moved into our new house at number 113 Childress Street at Sheppard AFB. This house was located between where Barbara and I first lived and where her mom and dad had lived when we were all stationed here in the 60's. Paul received a "Curve Ball" from above on the day the base delivered our furniture. The movers had brought the big bookcase into the house and placed it at the end of the hall. Ron and Robbie decided that the bookcase would be a really cool ladder. They tried to climb it. Just like Jack and Jill, Ron, Robbie and Otto came tumbling down. Otto did not survive the fall and we had to get Paul a new fish.

Sheppard AFB and the School of Health Care Sciences would be our home for the next four years since this was a fixed assignment. My next "Curve Ball" from above came in the form of "A" shift. We were assigned "A" shift by the "Powers That Be" and it devastated me at first. "A" shift ran from 0500 (5:00 am) until 1300 (1:00 pm). I would have to rise and shine by 3:30 am every day for the next four years. As in the past, my guiding forces took over and "A" shift turned out to be the best shift I have ever worked. I took up golf and would be on the base golf course by 1400 hours (2:00 pm) almost every day for my entire time at Sheppard. I became quite a good golfer during my tour of duty, but got burned out on golf after I left there. My greens fees were only nine dollars a month and I gladly paid those fees over the next four years. I bought a three-pack of golf balls every other day. They cost me more than my greens fees way back then.

Barbara was very understanding and never complained about me going to play every day. She has always spoiled me even more than my Aunt Roma and Aunt Anna Mae. My boss, Joe Nash, also took up golf. He and I played every day and became really good friends. We even took some of our classes on golf outings during down times and had a ball with instructor vs. student contests.

Having five children was a mixed bag for Barbara and me. We loved, and still love, all five of our children, but feeding, clothing and housing them was a bit over whelming. I may attempt to write a child rearing manual when I finish this book, as I do remember how such a book might have helped Barbara and me. I took a part-time job as a bartender at the Airmen's Club and Barbara got a job at the Base Exchange to help us make it through each month. We didn't have much time as a family during this period. It was really stressful for me and Barbara. Making it a kind of "Curve Ball" for us. Once again, my "Guiding Forces" moved in during the summer of 1973. Barbara and I would get a much needed break. Barbara's folks called in mid-May and asked if they could have all five kids come and stay with them in California for the summer. The folks had not seen the kids for a whole year and wanted some time to re-connect with them.

The day after school closed for the summer, I loaded all five kids into the trusty station wagon and headed west. Barbara could not get time off, so I drove them there by myself. What a trip. My next "Curve Ball" from above occurred on that trip. It appears that I was exceeding the legal speed limit as I traveled through Stanton, Texas. The Honorable Henry A. Gibson, Justice of the Peace, fined me one hundred and twenty five dollars for the error of my ways. I figured that I would pay the fine once I got back home and that Barbara really didn't need to be burdened with the minor details. I really didn't want to tell her, as she always said that I drive too fast.

During this time, we owned two cars for our family needs. The big station wagon belonged to Barbara. I drove a small Toyota with a five speed manual transmission that I used as my work car. All five kids plus luggage would not fit in the Toyota, so I left it for Barbara to drive while I took the kids to California. Barbara had no idea at all about how to shift gears and drive a manual shift car, but said she would try. I was gone for five days and Barbara never got my car out of second gear during that whole five day period. Some of my friends told me later that the Air Police at the main gate would see her coming and just wave her through so that she would not have to stop and change gears. Toyota made a great little car and mine survived its five days in second gear with no lasting side effects.

Barbara and I really grew close that summer. It was like the honeymoon we never had. We both still worked, but we had our evenings and weekends to ourselves. We even returned to Six Flags one weekend to see what it would be like without family. What I noticed most was how clean and quiet the house was without the kids. Shane (remember the dog) went crazy there all by himself all day. From June through August we only ate one meal at home and that was my fault. We had an inspector from Washington, D.C. come down to evaluate our program. I invited him over for a home cooked meal. Barbara would tease me about this for years to come.

Barbara's folks brought the kids back two days before the start of school. This would be our last alone time until all the kids were grown and gone from the house. It appears that Barbara's folks received a "Curve Ball" or two during that summer with the kids.

Dad's first words to me were, "Never again will we take all five at the same time."

He said that not a day went by that one or more of them wanted to go home to their dad. Barb's folks talked and laughed about that summer for many years to come.

When the kids got home, they all ran straight to Barbara yelling about the ticket that dad had gotten in Texas. I had to confess to Barbara about my incident in Stanton. Barbara loves being able to say, "I told you so."

She exercised that privilege every time we spoke about the kids' summer vacation in California. The woman never forgets any of the times I screwed up. It bothered me, at the time, the kids had ratted me out before they even said, "Hello" to either of us. It was like they knew that I would not tell Barbara about it and they were determined to see that justice was served.

During the remainder of my time at the School of Heath Care Sciences, I focused on improving myself academically. I earned my "Master Instructor" rating and attended all courses that the Air Force offered at the time. All of the training would pay off big time when I was finally able to attend college on a full-time basis.

When my transfer orders came in March of 1976, I was in the clouds. I was being re-assigned to Travis AFB and we would be able to see Barbara's folks a lot more often. I remember thinking that this assignment would be like going home in a way. Several of my former students had been assigned there and I still knew some people from my previous assignment. The only difference would be returning as the NCOIC.

Chapter 17
My Final Air Force assignment

It's ironic that I would begin my final Air Force assignment on April 1, 1976 (April Fool's Day). I was selected for the position of NCOIC (Non-Commissioned Officer in Charge) for the cardio-pulmonary department at David Grant Medical Center in Fairfield, California. I would serve in this position for the remainder of my time on active duty. Due to my position, I was offered and accepted base housing upon my arrival. This was great for the kids. They would all be able to attend school on the base. The twins would start school in August, so all five would be in school all day. We had a great four bedroom, two bath house just across the street from the Little League baseball fields.

During my final tour of duty, I was able to earn my bachelor's degree through a really great program offered by the Air Force. I hold a Bachelor of Science Degree in Occupational Education from Southern Illinois University. The university would send their professors to the base each weekend and I attended classes from 0800 to 1600 (8am to 4pm) both Saturdays and Sundays for over a year. The school gave me a bunch of credits for all of my Air Force training, so I did not need much to meet the requirements for graduation. The neat thing about this program was that the Air Force paid all of the bills. This included tuition, books and supplies. I had been taking courses at almost all of the bases and places we had been stationed, but this was the first time I was able to attend as a full-time student. I did very well and graduated with a 3.83 GPA.

The base was about a one hour drive into San Francisco, so I took the family there often. We became big fans of the Giants and attended a lot of baseball games every baseball season. Two of the guys who worked for me would usually go with us and the boys had a ball with them.

Jim Johnson and Peerless Williams were like uncles to my sons. The boys really liked them a lot. They liked to bet on the games with Jim and had many good times during and after games due to this wagering. Jim usually won and the boys would gladly pay up. Jim drank a lot of beer during the game, so the boys knew he would need to use the potty on the ride home. We had a really nice motor home at the time that had a bathroom on it. Paul would stand guard on the bathroom door and charge Jim a quarter every time he had to go. The boys usually came out ahead due to the many trips that Jim made to the bathroom.

I remember one Saturday when the Giants were having a father and son day at Candlestick Park. It was a chance to go down onto the field and meet with the coaches and players, get tips on how to play the game and collect autographs. We decided that Paul would be Peerless's son and that Ron (one of our identical twins) would be Jim's son for this event. Jim Johnson was a short, bald, mustached white guy who had no family resemblance and Peerless was a six foot four inch black man who had no family resemblance, but we were determined to make this work. The boys played long to the point that they were calling Jim and Peerless "Daddy" and we all got to go out on the field. I don't think that there was a player or coach who believed our family arrangements, but they all went along with it. I lost touch with Jim and Peerless over the years, but did read that Peerless died in 2012 at the age of 75. My boys still remember those trips to Candlestick Park and all the fun they had with their adopted dads.

Like every place we had ever been, I picked up a part-time job to help make ends meet. My life time "Curve Ball" has always been the time I lost with Barbara and the kids. I will always be happy that Barbara and I had/ have five children, but I regret all of the things I missed while they were growing up. We did, however, make the most of the time we did have. We did a lot together when I had the time. We would go camping in our motor home almost every weekend and the kids usually had a good time. We had several friends who also had campers. We would make weekend trips as a group. The kids had their friends and the adults could enjoy it and relax. I would tell my staff at the hospital that I would be out in the wilderness roughing it for the weekend and they would respond with comments about just how rough it would be in a motor home. I would respond by telling them that I would have to watch black and white TV all weekend.

I also made time, along with Jim and Peerless, to coach a Little League baseball team one summer. All three of my sons played for me and we had a great summer. Paul and I, because of our short fuses got thrown out of several ball games by the umpires. Barbara still has the boys' Little League pictures hanging in her office. I sneak a glance at them every time I go in there. I was also a Den Dad when Paul decided that he wanted to become a Cub Scout. Barbara also was an assistant in the Girl scouts for both Karla and Kari. Barbara was a big help to me on our Cub Scout meeting days at the house. She has always been into crafts and was always coming up with neat ideas for the Scouts to do. Paul and I also carved out a miniature racing car together. We entered it in a contest and got second place!

My next "Curve Ball" from above came in the form of some serious neck surgery. On the Sunday before Thanksgiving in 1977, I woke up with a very bad stiff neck, numbness in my right hand and pain like I had never felt before. I thought that I might have just slept on it the wrong way. Barbara thought that I was just faking it, so I could just sit around all day and watch football. The next morning it was worse and I went to see one of the orthopedic doctors at the hospital. After examining me, he sent me directly to see a neurosurgeon.

Doctor Moncrief admitted me to the hospital and scheduled surgery for the Friday after Thanksgiving. I don't have any idea how I might have done it, but I had shattered C6 and C7 in my spinal column. The doctor allowed me to go home for the day on Thanksgiving, but made me return to the hospital that evening to get prepared for surgery the next day. I did not know it at the time, but this surgery would grant me 50% disability when I retired from the Air Force. This meant that one half of my military retirement would be paid to me tax free and the way I looked at it, every little bit helps. The surgery went well and I have never suffered any after affects from it.

The day of my surgery was a very trying one for Barbara and her mother. Barbara's dad was undergoing triple by-pass heart surgery in Los Angeles at the same time I was having my neck surgery. I understand that they were on the phone most of the day with progress reports. Dad came through his surgery well and we both did fine later on. You know they say that men are the tough and strong ones in a relationship, but I am here to tell you that the women in my life were a lot stronger in the face of adversity than I would ever be. I have one tough lady.

I retired from active duty with the Air Force on September 1, 1979. I had honorably served my flag and my country for twenty years and ten days. I look back now and have a hard time believing it all went by so quickly. I would tell people that the twenty years went by really quickly, but the last ten days went on forever. I had enlisted when I was just seventeen, traveled the world, gotten married, had a family and little did I know, at that time, that I would be writing about it one day. I did not have a job when I retired, but did have appointments and prospects. My brother Bob talked us into settling in Oklahoma. He said that there were great job opportunities there, that it had a good housing market and really good schools for the kids. With all that, "Oklahoma here we come."

Chapter 18
Mustang, Oklahoma

We loaded up the full size van with the duel gas tanks at Barb's folks' house, said our good- byes and headed east to our new home. I loved driving back then and still do. I would end up driving straight through from Los Angeles to Oklahoma City. I had made a bed for the kids and the dog, Shane, between two of the rows of seats. They all slept while I drove on through the night with my duel gas tanks. I could go a long way in between stops with two gas tanks, so I covered as much distance as I could before I would stop. I couldn't do it today, as I am an old guy who must stop and pee every twenty miles or so. Barb would wake the kids and the dog whenever I stopped and advise them to answer natures' call while I gassed up. Having traveled with me in the past, they all knew to go now or forever hold your pee. I did pretty well on that trip. I made it all the way from Los Angeles to El Paso before I needed a rest. Barbara took over the driving for a couple of hours in the Texas Panhandle, but I took over and drove the rest of the way. Barbara insists on driving just at the speed limit or a couple of miles under, while I like to hammer down.

We arrived at my brother Bob's house on Labor Day of 1979 (Monday) about two hours before Monday night football. My beloved Pittsburgh Steelers were playing and would beat New England in that game. Barbara swears to this day that I drove straight through just to be able to watch that game. I imagine you have guessed by now that I am somewhat of a fan of the game of football. Barbara has a little knick-knack that she displays from August through February every year that reads: "This Marriage is on Hold for Football Season". I don't know where she bought it or where she keeps it, but it appears every year like clockwork. We would stay with Bob, his wife Sandy and her son Jimmy for about two weeks before we moved into our own house.

We bought our very first new house ever at 745 West Sheppard Drive in Mustang, Oklahoma in late September of 1979. We would keep that house until the year 2001. When we moved to Mustang, which is seventeen miles south west of Oklahoma City, the population was about 4,500 people. It has really grown over the years and the population today is over 40,000. It was a quiet little town when we moved there. It is a really nice place to raise a family. The housing addition was brand new, so all of our neighbors would become friends over the years. The kids all made friends there and all three boys still live there. This little house would end up serving nearly everyone in the family and would be the final home for Barbara's folks.

I was hired by the Pulmonary Services & Critical Care Unit at Oklahoma Memorial Hospital about two weeks after our arrival. I would work there until 1987. My education and Air Force experience landed this position for me and I will always be grateful to the Air Force for it. The hospital was the teaching hospital for the medical school at the University of Oklahoma. Some of my duties included training some third and fourth year medical students how to perform the procedures that we performed in our unit. My immediate supervisor was a guy by the name of Larry Troyer. Larry and I became really good and close friends. Larry re-introduced me to candied sweet potatoes that I had sworn off so many years before.

Now, that's a true friend!

The Chief of Medicine at the time was Doctor Robert (Bob) McCaffree.   At the time of this publication, he is still there working and teaching.   I really liked working there.   I had a lot of free time due to the Monday through Friday schedule that I worked. With this free time, I decided that it would be great to go back to school to try to earn a graduate degree.

With this new idea imbedded in my gray matter, it was all I could think of, but money was really tight back then.   I felt that I needed to get a part-time job to help make ends meet, but Barbara encouraged me to go to the Veterans Administration to see if they might help.   Following her advice, I went to the V.A. and learned that under the G.I. Bill, I would be paid to go to school.   There are those "Guiding Forces" again moving in and solving my problem of the day.   In addition to paying my tuition and buying my books and supplies, I was to receive a monthly check for over $500.00 for as long as I was in school.   Barbara and I would tell people that the V.A. made our house payments for the first eighteen months that we had our house.   I enrolled in a Master of Arts in Teaching program at Oklahoma City University in October of 1979.   I would graduate with my Master's degree in August of 1981.   My schedule was a real nightmare during the time I spent going to school.   I went to work at the hospital at 7:30 in the morning, got off work at 3:30 in the afternoon, drove over to the university, spent better than two hours in the library and then went to classes from six in the evening until ten Monday through Friday.   Mustang was over twenty miles from the university and it just wasn't feasible to go home before classes.   I give Barbara a lot of credit for all of the sacrifices she and the kids made during the time I was enrolled in school.   She had to be the mom, the dad, chauffeur and all around jack-of-all-trades while I played student. I owe a lot of my success in school to her and the kids. I spent as much time as I could with Barb and the kids on the weekends and tried to make it up to them for the times I wasn't there. The kids were growing up and I was missing out on an awful lot of it. I don't know how she did it, but Karla turned sixteen and started driving a car. The last time I saw her, she was jumping rope in the driveway. I do remember going to a car dealer on my graduation day, in my cap and gown, to buy her the very first car she would own. She and her mom certainly do like RED and her first car was a red Mercury Cougar.

My next "Curve Ball" from above came in the fall of 1983 when I learned by way of the telephone that Karla was pregnant. The really bad part was that it was by a guy I really didn't like and had forbidden her to see or date. I am one of the nicest and most easy going guys on the planet, but at that moment I became a monster who even frightened me. I immediately went to the store where this coward worked, but he had heard that I was coming for him and had taken off for the rest of the day. I am certain that if he had been there that I would have hurt him badly. I would have probably gotten into some really heavy duty legal problems. Barbara and Karla had both warned him that I was headed his way and they made arrangements to meet with him and his parents that evening. I came away from that meeting knowing that if I ever meet the coward again that I will punch him in his face. During our discussion, while he hid behind his mother, he stated that he would help to take care of the baby if we could prove that it was his. I wanted to really hurt this SCUM and repay him for hurting Karla, but to be honest, I don't know if I could have taken his mother. She was more of a man than her son would ever be. I have never seen this slime ball again since that evening in his living room. Just as in the past, those "Guiding Forces" in my life delivered to all of us Jessica Dawn Kimmel on March 28, 1984. She was then, is now, and will always be the light of our lives. We all love her more than what can be expressed by words.

We converted our garage into a bedroom/nursery for mommy and baby Jessica. I remember buying her a stuffed toy from the gift shop at the hospital every day for the first month after she was born. My secretary, Janie Kimmet, bought me a bumper sticker that read: "If I had known that being a grandparent was so much fun, I would have done it first" and I think that I may still have it in a box somewhere around here.

Barbara's mom and dad moved from California to Oklahoma to care for Jessica while we all worked. They really loved her and spent every day for the first three years of her life seeing her every day. In June of 1984, our daughter Kari graduated from Mustang High School. The whole family attended the graduation. The coward's mother sent her daughter over to ask if she might come over and see and hold Jessica. I told you she had more balls than her son. I graciously consented, provided she could kill me and step over my dead body. I know that you are not supposed to hold a grudge, but this woman had not earned the right to see or to hold my terrific grand-daughter. Karla would eventually take Jessica to see her and the coward against my strongest objections. I can only hope that the love that we all gave to Jessica made up some for not having a daddy.

Kari was responsible for my next "Curve ball" from above when she announced that she was going to forego a scholarship offer and move to California with her best friend Jennifer. I was so angry with her that I did not speak with her for over a year. She has since gone back to school and earned her degree. She finally realized that having to work three jobs just to make ends meet in California was just not worth it and moved back home in 1986. I remember coming home from work and her popping out of the hallway closet to surprise me. It was one of the very best surprises that I have ever received. Jennifer remained in California and got married shortly after Kari returned home. Kari and Jennifer are still good friends and they try to get together when they can. All I knew was that it was good to be a whole family again. We had all five kids at home. Jessica lived with us and Barbara's mom and dad were five minutes and three streets away. It sort of reminded me of how good it was when I was living with my grandparents and how good it felt to have family around. Bob and Sandy had even moved to Mustang and we saw a lot of them during this time.

Barbara had a great job with the U.S. Immigration and Naturalization Service. I had been selected as the supervisor at the hospital when Larry Troyer resigned to go out on his own. It appeared that we were set for life. In early 1987, I had an experience that would change our lives forever. I went to work one morning and was told that one of our long time patients had passed away during the night. His passing really hit me hard and caused me to rethink about what I wanted to do for the rest of my life. I came to the realization that I had been caring for very seriously ill patients for over twenty five years and that maybe it was to for me to do something else. I think that I was tired of seeing people die and not be able to do anything about it. I had always dealt with patients with chronic heart and lung problems and had lost count of the number that I had seen pass away. What was ironic, in this case, was that I could barely remember the man who had died, but could see and remember all of his family members who had come to see him on a daily basis. It appeared that it might be time to look for another way to make a living.

Hello! The "Guiding Forces" in my life stepped in once again and saved the day for me. In March of 1987, the U.S. Immigration and Naturalization Service had just initiated an amnesty program involving several million illegal immigrants and they were in desperate need of temporary hire employees to meet their needs for this program. As fate would have it, there was going to be a legalization office in Oklahoma City. Barbara arranged an interview for me. The officer in charge, Jim Walsh, hired me on the spot provided I passed the government background check. I went to work for U.S. INS on April 20, 1987 as a GS-7 Step 1 Legalization Adjudicator. Jim was a good supervisor, leader and mentor. He encouraged all of us to work hard and to apply for permanent positions as they became available.   He was constantly reminding us that our positions were only temporary and that we would one day be out of a job.

One day in July, I came to work and found an announcement for immigration inspectors throughout the country, along with a note from Jim telling me to apply. I followed his suggestion and filled out and mailed in the application forms. I was contacted on a Monday morning in early October. I was instructed to report to Atlanta the following Friday for an interview for the position of immigration inspector. My next "Curve Ball" from above was the fact that Barbara and I could not afford a plane ticket to Atlanta for this interview and it appeared that I was going to have to call these people and decline. Fate and Jim Walsh intervened. Arrangements were made for me to have a telephone interview. The telephone interview took place at the same time on Friday that I was scheduled to be there. I was interviewed by the port director and two of the first line supervisors. I felt really confident both during and after the interview. When I got off the phone, Jim asked me how I did, and I said, "I am headed to Atlanta."

I was notified the following Monday morning that I had been selected and I was given a December reporting date. I will always be grateful to Jim Walsh for all that he did for me while I worked for him and for all that he did to help me secure the Atlanta job.

Chapter 19
Welcome to Atlanta

I arrived in Atlanta the Sunday before Christmas of 1987. I would be there by myself until July of 1988. This was the longest and most "Curve Ball" filled seven months that I have ever experienced. During this period, my oldest son Paul got married and our twins Ron and Rob graduated from high school. I missed a wedding anniversary and a tornado and hail storm hit our house in Mustang. Talk about "Curve Balls" and of felling helplessness. I know that I have said this before, but the best and most wonderful thing in my life was and is Barbara. She came through all of these "Curve Balls" with flying colors. She managed the house, the kids and all the other trials and tribulations like the trooper that she is. Her strength and courage makes me look like the biggest sissy on the planet. She will always be my rock. The worst day in that seven months was Christmas Day. I was so far away from home and family. Barbara called me three times that day and we both cried harder each time she called.

From December through March, I worked as an inspector trainee. I took to inspections like a duck takes to water. It was like this was what I was born to do for the rest of my life. By the time I left for formal training at the Federal Law Enforcement Training Center (FLETC), I was spending the majority of my inspection time doing interviews in the secondary inspection area. This is where the line inspectors send the suspected bad guys for further questioning and examination of them and their belongings. My lifetime "Guiding Forces" had led me to my new calling.   I was destined for a fine career number three with the Immigration and Naturalization Service as an inspector.

I attended the Federal Law Enforcement Academy from March of 1988 through June of 1988.   I can honestly say that it was the most demanding training I have ever gone through.   I remember the first day at the center and being called to attention for the officer in charge as he entered the auditorium.   Mr. Murphy ordered us to look to our right and then to look to our left and then he said, "Those people you just looked at will not be here when you graduate."

He stated that only the very best of us would make it through the training.   It was a scare tactic that he used to get our attention and to keep us focused for what lay ahead of us.

We started out with 44 students in our class and only graduated 32.   We lost twelve of our classmates through failure in either academic, physical or firearms training arenas.   I remember very well the first two students that we lost.   It was an event that woke up the whole class.   We had taken an Immigration Law Examination in the morning, had two other classes and then went to lunch.   As we began our first class of the afternoon session, our course advisor and another instructor came into the classroom with very solemn looks on their faces.   Pointing at the two guys who had failed the exam they said, "You and you pack your bags. Both of you have failed the test and are gone."

By the time we returned to the dorm after class, their rooms were empty and their beds had been stripped. We would be witness to this event several more time throughout the course, but my roommate and I were determined that we were going to make it through to graduation. Jim Derbyshire and I set up a routine that we followed religiously for our entire time at the school. We went to breakfast every morning, attended all classes, took good notes and stayed focused. Classes were over at four in the afternoon and Jim and I would be back in our room by 4:30. Jim would make a pot of coffee while we watched Divorce Court on Jim's portable TV. After Divorce Court, we would take our coffee out on to the balcony, smoke a cigarette and then go to dinner at five. After dinner, we would smoke one more cigarette on the balcony and get ready to study. We studied every day Monday through Friday from six until eight and were in bed by nine every school night. We knew that getting a good night's sleep was important and we NEVER burned the mid-night oil like some of our classmates. This paid off for us, as we were always well rested and well prepared for all of our tests. We had five people going through from Atlanta and all five of us graduated. I was really a proud puppy the day I drove out of the gates of FLETC. After I finished my post academy required training, I would be an immigration inspector.

I found a really great house for us in Riverdale, Georgia when I returned from the academy. I was ready to move Barbara and the family to our new duty station. Barb had been notified that the district office was giving her a "Spouse Transfer" and that she would have a job waiting for her when she arrived. The house in Riverdale had three bedrooms, was in a great location near the airport and had a basement apartment for Karla and Jessica. Barb's folks had moved back to Indiana, and Paul and his wife Paula (Paul and Paula, it sounds like the song of the same name) were going to move into our house in Mustang. In addition to Karla and Jessica, the twins would be moving to Georgia with us. I was really happy that I would have someone to come home to and that we would be a family again. It appeared that we would all be settled in nicely, even though we would not all be in the same location. Barb's folks were renting a house from a widow whose husband had recently died and she told them that they could stay there for as long as they wanted to. Keep this in mind, as Barb's folks will be receiving a "Curve Ball" of their own during the time they rented this house.

We moved into the house in Riverdale in the middle of July of 1988. Both Barbara and I went back to our respective places of employment with the INS. Barbara rode with me to the airport every day, and then took the train into her job in Atlanta. Karla got a job in a daycare and we were all on our way to getting settled into our new life in Georgia.

Our next "Curve Ball" came about a year later when Paul and Paula decided to buy and move into their own house. They could not have picked a worse time. The housing market was in the toilet at the time. I could not have sold the house in Mustang for what I owed on it and it appeared that we would be paying rent in Georgia and a house payment in Oklahoma on an empty house. We were in a real pickle for about three months. We kept hoping and praying that the market would get better or that something would come along to get us out of this situation.

Barbara's mom called one evening crying and all upset about their place in Indiana. It appeared that the widow lady had found a boyfriend and wanted to move back into her house by the first of the next month. Barb's folks were at their wits end and had no idea about what they would do. Their problem and ours was solved when Barbara and I offered them our house in Mustang rent free. They still had a lot of friends, Paul, Paula, Kari and her family in Oklahoma, so they agreed. Ron and I flew to their place in Indiana, rented a U-Haul and moved the folks back to Oklahoma.

On November 29, 1989 we received a call from Kari telling us that she had gone into labor and was about to give birth. Barbara and Ron jumped into her car and set out for Oklahoma. Casey Scott Butler was born the next day and I would have my very first grandson. I remember getting a call from Kari from her hospital bed telling me that she was holding Casey. I could hear him in the background making some kind of squeaky noise and I tagged him with the nick-name of Squeaky on the spot. I called him Squeaky for a long time, but later changed it to C.B. which sounded and is much cooler.

Kari and her family bought a house two doors away from Barb's folks a couple of years later and Casey (C.B.) would pay them surprise visits all the time. Kari even taught Casey how to dial Nana's phone number and he would call her a hundred times a day to see how and what she was doing. Barbara's folks would live in the little house in Mustang for the remainder of both their lives.

I really like working at the airport as an inspector, but didn't see much opportunity for advancement. At that time, the journeyman inspectors only went to GS-9's. The only way to become a GS-11 was through getting promoted to the position of Supervisory Inspector (SII). Two of the three SII's at that time were from Atlanta and the third had just relocated there with his school-age children. Immigration examiners had a GS-11 journeyman level, so I applied for an examinations position with the Atlanta district. I was accepted as an immigration examiner trainee and began training in naturalizations, adjustments and marriage fraud cases. I really liked doing marriage fraud cases and caught several bad guys during my time with that unit. I earned a really cool nick-name during the time I spent in examinations and lived up to it every chance I got. They called me "The King of Denial" and it had nothing to do with the river in Egypt. I denied more applications than anyone else in the office. I had one case that was really gratifying to me and always remember it and its end result. I had a couple applying to adjust the husband from a conditional resident to a permanent resident which is based on the fact that the U.S. citizen and applicant have can prove that they have resided with one another over a two year period. They do this with copies of utility bills, rent receipts, tax returns or any paperwork that shows that they have been together over the required period of time.

This particular couple really looked good on paper, as they had receipts that were in both names, tax returns and all of the things that would prove that they were living together as husband and wife. I noticed on the tax return that there were six names of children and their ages and that they were being claimed as deductions. The conditional resident told me UNDER OATH that these were the names and ages of his brothers and sisters and that he helped his parents with their support. I informed the couple that I was going to send a request to the American Embassy in the man's home country and request that they verify what the man was telling me under oath was, in fact, true. When the report came back, it told me that the man had a wife and that the children listed on the tax return were his. This is what I had suspected. I called the couple back into the office a week or so later for a follow up interview. When they returned to my office, I interviewed them one at a time with the lying husband coming in first. He confessed to me that he had lied to me and that his U.S. citizen wife did not know that he was already married and that the children were his. I then called the wife in, showed her the report from the embassy and told her what the husband had said. Before I could say or do anything, she had him on the floor of my office. She would have strangled him if I had not stepped in. I can still see his eyes bugging out and the terror he had on his face.

The assignment at the district meant that Barbara and I could drive to work together, have lunch every day and kind of get reacquainted. I like to think of this assignment as a reward for the seven months that we had been separated at the beginning of my Atlanta assignment. We did encounter a joint "Curve Ball" once every year that we were stationed in Atlanta. We were separated on our wedding anniversary (June 22) in 1989, 1990 and 1991. I was in training at the academy in 1989, on an emergency detail to Charleston, South Carolina during the Panama Crises in 1990 and on a legalization detail to Tifton, Georgia in 1991.

At one point, Barbara asked my boss if I was paying him to send me away every year in June. We just recently celebrated our 50th wedding anniversary, so I would venture to say that we did not suffer any lasting ill effects from the ones that we missed. In July of 1991, we were both accepted for positions with the Southern Service Center (SSC) in Dallas, Texas. Very soon we would be close enough to be able to visit the family in Oklahoma.

Our final Atlanta "Curve Ball" was when Karla informed us that she and Jessica would be staying in Georgia. Karla had a good job, Jessica liked her school and they had both made some really good and close friends. Leaving them behind was one of the most difficult things we'd have ever had to do. One of the most difficult things for any parent or grandparent is to let go. We all cried like babies as we said our so-longs, but it really was time for them to be on their own. They are both married now and still live in and call Georgia their home.

Chapter 20
Dallas, Texas 1991-1994

Barbara and I signed in at the Southern Service Center on August 20, 1991.   It was Barbara's birthday. Barbara was assigned as the supervisor for the Freedom of Information Section and I was assigned to the L-Petition Unit of the examinations branch. We were personally welcomed by Sam Martin who was the Officer in Charge and by Jim Bruzinski who was Sam's assistant. Sam Martin was the very best supervisor for which I would ever work. I would model my own supervisory style after his.   Sam believed in hiring good people, letting them know what was expected of them and then letting them do their jobs. He always made himself available, but never over managed any of his people.

You could and would see him and his red suspenders all over the building singing the latest Garth Brooks' song. He did more for morale and harmony in the work place than anyone I have ever met. I worked very hard during the time I spent at the SSC and received my very first cash bonus at rating time.   Denise Ogden was my first line supervisor and she was a joy to work for. She arranged for me to go to examiner journeyman training in Artesia, New Mexico. She was equally as supportive as Sam and Jim. We also made some new friends at the SSC when we hooked up with Lee and Claudia Livingston. Lee, Claudia, Barbara and I all arrived at the SSC at the same time. We became instant friends. We have remained friends and still have a meal or two together every week to this day.

We received a devastating "Curve Ball" on July 10,

1992 when Barbara's dad passed away at the age of 72. He had had a stroke and suffered from headaches and some knee problems related to the time he was a P.O.W. The one thing that I will always be grateful for was our transfer from Atlanta to Dallas because we were able to visit and spend time with him during the final year of his life. The one thing I was really sorry about was that he was not alive when I got my SII position at DFW. I know that he was up there looking down on me during the selection process and I feel, in my heart, that he helped me get it. We have a picture of Barbara's folks in our living room and I find myself talking to them even now asking for advice or just telling them how much I miss them. I actually knew Barbara's dad longer than I knew my own father and we became as close as father and son (I miss you Dad).

I really liked the SSC, but I missed being in uniform and the excitement of inspections. I applied for a supervisory immigration inspector position at DFW (Dallas-Fort Worth International Airport) and waited for what seemed like an eternity for a reply.

Sam Martin ordered me to his office on August 21st and I was worried that I had done something wrong. I had never been ordered to report to Sam before. Sam started his conversation with the following way, "In spite of what I told them about you, they selected you anyway."

With a big smile on his face, he congratulated me on being selected for the SII position at DFW. I reported to DFW on August 26, 1992. I still consider it as one of the very best birthdays I have ever had. This was my very first assignment as a supervisor with immigration and I prayed really hard that I would do well and be worthy of the trust and faith that had been placed in me.

DFW was a great assignment and for the second time in my working career I would be working for a guy by the name of Bob Schultz. Bob was a great supervisor. He gave us a free hand with our assigned duties. Barbara said that his language needed to be cleaned up, but she really liked him. Bob was a helicopter jockey in Viet Nam. In my opinion, he could talk anyway he wanted to. Bob only had to give me the Bob Schultz evil eye one time during my tour of duty at DFW. One of my jobs, when flights were in, was to keep the people moving down to Customs. We had a small area and it could become congested very easily. One day a U.S. Citizen was standing around waiting for a foreign associate and I had asked him three times to please move on to Customs. When I asked him the fourth time, he told me to stop harassing him and that he was paying my salary. This was the one remark that we did not want to hear coming from a passenger regardless of who they were. I forgot that Bob was standing next to me when I told this guy, "You don't pay me enough to put up with --- holes like you."

Bob took me to his office and really cracked up after he chewed my butt out pretty good. The one thing that I really liked about Bob was that he said what was on his mind, and you always got the straight scoop from him. We would have made lousy politicians. I was assigned as the supervisor over training and supplies as my collateral duties. I was determined to do the very best job I could. Angel McKinny was my supply assistant and she did an outstanding job for me. She kept me out of trouble that first year and we never ran out of anything. Angel would be my first line supervisor some years later and we would once again work well together. Dennis Silva was the training officer at the time and he was doing a pretty good job.   He was really focused on firearms training and it appeared to me that he placed too much emphasis on guns and not enough on the education and training of our troops. Thanks to Dennis, we had a first class shooting range and were among the first in INS to have moving targets.   Dallas and DFW were really starting to grow at that time and it was exciting to be a part of that growth.   According to Angel, J.T. Lawson, Mickey Rowell, Greg Moore, Karen Hagman and Denise Blackwell, I was doing a pretty good job at my first go at being an INS Supervisor.

Denise Blackwell and I had a minor disagreement on my rating of her in that first year, but we got through and over it.   Denise had been receiving outstanding on all elements of her performance from all of her past supervisors, but only received an excellent from me.   I called her into my office and allowed her to read her evaluation.   After reading what I had written, she refused to sign it, as was her privilege.   She came back to me an hour later and pointed out some good work she had done in one particular area and I agreed with her that she had done excellent work in that area.   She tried this tactic with me several more times and I again agreed that she had done excellent work.   She finally said, "You are not going to change my rating are you?"

I then told her that she had done excellent work for me.   She signed the form and we have been good friends since that day.   I would work with both Denise and her husband in another location a few years later.

As I reflect on my days at DFW and the very fine staff officers I had, I get a very real sense of pride. All of these young officers would rise to some very important positions and serve both INS and CBP. They would help to make it a better organization.   I like to think that I might have taught them a little about what supervision was all about and that they might have carried a little of what they learned from me with them on their career journeys.

In March of 1994, I applied for several positions for port directors at various locations throughout the INS. The majority of these positions were posted as GS-12/1, and meant that you could be selected as a GS-12 and work your way up to GS-13. I told Barbara that I was applying for these positions just to see how I might do on this type of list. I had only been with INS for a short period of time and I expected that it would probably take me a little while longer to advance. Back in those days, you were told where you stood on any list even though you may not have been selected. It gave you an idea of where you might need to improve upon. In reality, I did not expect to be selected for any of the positions for which I had applied, but felt that I might get a good idea about areas in which I could improve. What I did not factor into my thinking was the fact that I held a Master's Degree. This was held in high regard because of the value the selection boards placed on education. As it turned out, I was the only applicant with a graduate degree.

I was assigned as the duty supervisor at terminal A at DFW on July 4, 1994. I was on the 0500 to 1300 shift (5am to 1pm). One day, two inspectors had called in sick and I was manning an inspection booth until a replacement arrived. Bob Schultz came into my booth and said that he would relieve me so that I could take a phone call that had come in for me. I thought it might be Barbara or one of the troops, so I went to take the call. The call turned out to be from Donald Radcliff, who was the district director for the Hawaii District. He was calling to inform me that I had been selected as the Area Port Director in Guam.

For the first time in my life, I was at a loss for words. I stood there for a while not saying a word and some of the troops began asking me if something was wrong. I thanked Mr. Radcliff for the personal call, accepted the position and swore to him that I would do a good job for him. He congratulated me again and told me that the Guam Officer in Charge would be calling me at home that evening. I don't remember too much more about that shift after the call from Mr. Radcliff.

I received a call from Guam that evening around 8:00 pm, and it was the surprise call of a lifetime. The Officer in Charge was Sam Martin and I was going to have the honor and privilege of working for him once again. Sam had taken the OIC job in Guam because the previous OIC, AOIC and Port Director had all been relieved of their respective duties. They were all being investigated for some sort of improprieties. Sam was charged with rebuilding the office and port. Sam told me that he was in the process of creating a position for which Barbara could apply, but that it would take a little time. He also told me that he needed and wanted me to report for duty as soon as possible. Due to the circumstances, there would be no delays in financing my move and getting me reassigned to Guam. When Sam finished talking with me, he talked to Barbara about Guam and about the position he was working on for her. Little did we know, at that time, but we would have another long separation. At least there was no anniversary involved.

I learned from Bob Schultz the next day that Sam had called two weeks before to get Bob's recommendation on me. Bob also told me that I was really the man Sam wanted for that job. Greg Moore,

Angel McKinney, J.T. Lawson, Denise Blackwell and the rest of the DFW troops threw me one of the very best farewell parties I have ever had. Collectively, this was the finest group of men and women I had or ever would have to supervise. They were the hardest working, dedicated and loyal group I would ever have the pleasure of knowing. Fortunately for me, we would all cross paths again during our careers and we all still keep in touch through Angel.

Barbara and I made arrangements for Ron and Rob to stay with Paul and Paula. We made certain that Barbara's mom would have everything she needed. Mom was really independent, had a lot of friends at church and in the neighborhood and would do just fine. She really did pretty well for the first six months or so that we were gone. She and her friends would go to Bingo a couple of times a week and she stayed busy with the house and at church.

Barbara would need to make all of the arrangements to ship the household items, sell the house in Arlington and get the family situated. She handled it a lot better than I could have if I were the one left behind. Ron and Rob were going to take my truck with them to Oklahoma, so their transportation problems were solved. Barbara would end up buying and shipping a really beautiful silver Mustang Convertible as her car. We drove that car all over Guam, usually with the top down and the radio blasting. It amazes me that I still had and do have Barbara after all of the moves I have made and all the times I left her with the bulk of the physical responsibilities. She is a real trooper.

Chapter 21
Haifa Dai from Guam

I reported to the Hawaii district office on August 22, 1994 for official processing for my position in Guam. I would spend the first three days of my Guam assignment in Hawaii. The district office housed me in the Waikiki Hilton on the eighth floor overlooking the Pacific Ocean. For the next three mornings, I would have my morning coffee on my lanai and watch the sun come up over Diamond Head. I had several meetings with the D.D. and his staff, went through all of my processing and prepared to go to Guam. I had a really nice three days in Hawaii and took in a lot of the places that attract tourists.

My next "Curve Ball" came on the day I was to fly to Guam. The Continental ticket agent was not going to allow me to carry my service weapon with me on board the plane. He wanted me to put it in my checked bag, which he would identify as carry a weapon. He planned to do this be placing a large, bright orange sticker to the bag with the words "firearm inside" on it. I wondered which baggage handler would go home that night with my gun in their possession. My personal weapon was a 357 Magnum Colt Python that I had been authorized to carry by the INS as my service weapon and this clown wanted me to put it into a marked bag. While we were discussing the issue, the pilot approached and asked what the problem was. I showed the Captain my orders, my gun carrying case and explained that as a federal officer I was authorized to carry my weapon on my person at all times. The pilot asked me if I would have any problem putting my weapon in my backpack and the cartridges in my briefcase. I agreed and he gave me permission to carry my weapon on board. He even had the ticket agent upgrade me to first class.

I arrived in Guam on the evening of August 26, 1994. Yes, I would be beginning my new assignment on my birthday! Sam Martin and my old roommate Jim Derbyshire met me at the plane and expedited me through Guam's Immigration and Customs. Several comments were made about my Colt and I think that some of the Guam customs officers were trying to figure out a legal way in which to confiscate my gun. Sam and Jim took me to the Princess Hotel (Guam's finest at the time). They got me settled in for the night. Sam made arrangements to pick me up bright and early the next day and give me a briefing before taking me to the airport. I only stayed in the Princess for two days before moving into the Alophong Beach Towers. This move was made possible by Lynn Palasios who was from Guam and the AOIC. I had known Lynn from a detail I had in Artesia a few years earlier and we were good friends. Lynn was a great first line and she gave me glowing evaluations the entire time she rated me. I spent the remainder of August, all of September and October in the Alophong, but moved when my per diem ran out. I stayed in the Navy Bachelor Officers Quarters (BOQ) from then until my housing became available. I landed a really nice three bedroom house at 32 Golden Shower Circle in Dededo, Guam. Barbara and I would live there for my entire tour of duty in Guam.

It turned out to be somewhat of a "Curve ball" for the night shift inspectors when I first arrived. My predecessor was somewhat of a slacker and had allowed the first line supervisors and troops to run the port as they saw fit. I have always been an early riser and would sometimes get to my office at two or three in the morning. This seemed like an excellent way to was going on. The very first day I showed up at the airport (3:00 am), I found half of the shift asleep and the other half working. Passengers filled the hall and were having to wait in long lines due to this situation. We were the Immigration and Naturalization Service and it appeared to me that this shift had taken the word service out of the equation.

I learned that this midnight to eight shift was staffed with all volunteers and that they had arranged among themselves to alternate nights of sleeping and working. On this particular evening, even the first line supervisor was asleep. The **it hit the fan when I learned of it. This practice came to a screeching halt. I had the supervisor and staff on the carpet at the end of that shift. The supervisor was from Guam and owned a small farm that he worked during the day because he was well rested from the night before. Another one of the troops had a real estate job that she worked every other day. Get the every other day picture? One of my very first official duties as the Area Port Director was breaking up this merry band of people and making certain that the U.S. tax payers were getting their money's worth from these employees. I was not the most popular man in Guam during this period in my career.

Guam was the most diverse assignment that I had or ever will have. I had around 80 officers on staff at the time and one administrative assistant. One half of the staff were state-side hires and the other half were local hires. The local hires did not care for the state-side hires, as they felt as though they were taking jobs away from the locals. When I took over, I had brothers, sisters, cousins, uncles, husbands, wives and all sorts of people who were related in one way or another among the local hires. The local hires were comprised of Guamanians and Filipinos and these two factions did not get along very well. My first "Curve Ball" came as a result of this division. Shortly after my arrival, I was approached by one of my female officers who was going to have a baby. She was requesting to be put on a permanent day shift until the baby came. She was a good worker and the request was logical, so I granted her request and told the scheduling supervisor to make the necessary changes in the schedule. Less than one week later, I was summoned to Sam Martin's office to address a letter of complaint which he had received. The letter complained that I was showing favoritism toward the Filipino officers. The female officer who was pregnant was a Filipino. Sam was not at all upset and let me handle the situation in my own manner. I held a mandatory meeting of all officers and supervisors. I had no idea who belonged to which faction and I did not care what their backgrounds were. I told them that I believed in equal opportunity and that I did not and would not show favoritism to any group. I also asked that they might want to come to me or their first line supervisor before initiating letters. Sophie ended up on her permanent shift and a month or so later gave birth to a really cute little girl.

I moved into 33 Golden Shower on December 3, 1994. Barbara would arrive one week later. The Navy even provided furniture for this house until our things arrived. Jim and Martha Derbyshire lived at 31 Golden Shower and would be our neighbors until we all departed Guam. There was a Navy chaplain and his family who lived in between me and Jim. All of the houses were in five or six house cul-de-sacs and we all became close. It was a nice three bedroom house that was only ten minutes from the airport. In addition to getting the house, I also bought a car. I purchased a white Ford Mustang Convertible a couple of years older than Barbara's car. We were going to be a two convertible family. My personal life was starting to fall into place and all I needed was for Barbara to get there.   After all of her trials and tribulations during the move over the past four months of separation, Barbara finally arrived on December 10, 1994.   We would be together for Christmas.   Even though we would have to celebrate without our family, it was one of the nicest holidays we have ever had. As I recall, we didn't do a whole lot, but we were together.

There were two military installations on Guam at that time.   Both had great exchanges and commissaries. The biggest problem we had was that almost everyone on Guam had shopping privileges at both.   If you saw something you wanted you had better buy it right then.   When I first arrived on Guam, I made the mistake a couple of times of saying that I would get it the next time I came. Every time when I went back, the item was gone. When you live on an island, the first thing you must keep in mind is that all goods are brought in and are usually in limited supply.

Barbara arrived in Guam on the evening of December 10, 1994, but all of our household things would not arrive until sometime in January. Barbara was bound and determined that she and I would decorate our new house for Christmas to include a Christmas tree. We drove to Anderson AFB bright and early the next morning in search of a tree with all the trimmings. We were able to buy a really nice seven foot unlighted tree, four boxes of assorted ornaments and the very last two boxes of icicles. We then drove all the way to the south end of the island to the Navy Exchange in search of lights for our new Christmas tree.   There were no lights to be had at the main exchange or at the special Christmas annex that had been stocked for the holiday. At that time there were no K-Marts or Wal-Marts on Guam, but we tried every department and novelty store on the island to no avail. It appeared that we were going to have a tree that would probably be nice to look at during the day, but would not be lit in the evening. We took our purchases to the house and were feeling a little let down about our lighting situation.   As we were unloading the car, one of our other neighbors came over to introduce themselves and commented about the Christmas decorations. We told her about the problem we had in finding lights and she told us that Kentucky Fried Chicken was giving away a string of lights with the purchase of its ten piece meals. Since it was lunch time, we went to KFC, bought a ten piece meal and received our first string of colored lights for our tree. We went to KFC for the next six nights straight from work and ended up with almost enough lights for our tree. I did not touch KFC for the remainder of our time on Guam. I don't really go there much even today. As I remember it, we ate chicken for all three meals for the first week after Barbara arrived. When we look back on it, we always laugh and remember that particular Christmas with a certain fondness. After all of the chicken we had eaten to get our lights, we settled on a ham for our Christmas dinner. We spent part of the day with Jim and Martha. Throughout the day, several of the troops and their families stopped by to wish us a Merry Christmas.

Guam became a U.S. territory due to the spoils of war after the Spanish-American War. The original and current inhabitants are Chamorro and speak that language. Some of the first U.S. settlers on the island were Catholic Monks who brought with them the Catholic religion.   Guam is over 90% Catholic even today and each village has a patron saint.

My next "Curve Ball" was due to one of the villages' celebrations of its patron saint holiday. Shortly after my arrival, I was approached by inspector Herb Gofigan and invited to attend one villages' celebration of their patron saint on the upcoming weekend. I graciously accepted Herb's kind offer. I was looking forward to experiencing some of the local culture. Later on in my tour, Barbara and I would attend the wedding feast of Herb's daughter. It appeared that at least one of the villages would be celebrating (having a fiesta) almost every weekend. My invitations to these events began to flow like wine. Since I had accepted Herb's invitation, I felt a certain obligation to attend every time I was invited.   The people of Guam are the kindest, sweetest and most generous people on the planet. They really know how to grill chicken and roast a whole pig.   The fiestas usually ran from Thursday or Friday through the weekend. They were filled with great food, the most wonderful music you have ever heard with dancing and singing.   Their warmth and fellowship was like nothing you have never seen. My "Curve Ball" was that if I stayed on Guam too long, I would need a bigger house, bed, car and clothes because of all of the weight I was gaining. We also had great parties at the airport and at the homes of the staff celebrating a variety of events.

Barbara and I decided to throw a Valentine's Day party at our house. We invited both the airport and downtown INS people. It was the custom, in Guam at the time, to advertise your event with some sort of flyer describing the event. I put one together that looked like it was put together by a two year old just learning how to write and draw. Sean Kurdish, one of my troops who knew his way around a computer, volunteered to make one for me that I would be proud to use. I definitely could use the assistance from an expert. My flyer was supposed to read: Happy Valentine's Day, Celebrate Sweetheart's Day by bringing someone near and dear. It went on to give the time, date, location and other information about the party. As I have stated, my flyer looked like it was done by someone with severe learning disabilities. It was so bad that Sean could not read some of what I had written and Sean's first flyer ended up reading: Bring someone neat and clean. We corrected it before we made copies and invited people to the party. I spoke with Sean a few months ago and we always end our conversations with the statement "Bring someone neat and clean" as it has become a little bit of a joke with us. No one, but Sean or I, has ever know about this error until it appeared here in this book.

Guam would be the very first time I would have an administrative assistant and I had the nicest, sweetest, easy going and efficient in all of Guam. Her name was Bernadette Mayoyoy. She was the most efficient and hardworking employee on the staff including me. Bernadette made certain that I was where I was supposed to be at the appointed time. She even went so far as to stick her head in my office door at exactly twelve noon each day and announce, "Mr. Kimmel, its noodle time" and then she would go back to her desk. I was hooked on Cup-O-Noodle at the time and brought one every day for lunch. Bernadette noticed me carrying my unused ones back home a couple of times and made it one of her official duties to remind me to stop working and eat lunch. She was really a great secretary and I always think about her when I have any kind of soup.

We received a "Curve Ball" in May when we received a phone call from Paul telling us that Nana (Barb's mom) was ill. Barbara took leave and went home to care for her. It turned out that one of her medications was not doing what it was supposed to and after a change of medication she was fine. Robbie came back to Guam with Barbara and stayed with us for the remainder of our tour of duty in Guam.

We had gotten a kitten that was supposed to frighten away the dreaded Guam Brown Tree Snake which inhabits the island. Rob has always loved and still does love all kinds of animals, but he has always been more of a dog lover than cat lover. He actually taught that darn cat to fetch a ball like a dog. I think that with a little more time he might have had her barking like one.

Barbara was always a little nervous and was worried about her mom after her return to Guam. With this in mind, I began applying for positions a little closer to Oklahoma.   I was selected for an assistant port director position in Miami in February of 1996 and would soon be leaving Guam. By this time, Sam Martin and Lynn had gotten things turned around downtown and the airport was running smoothly.

Jim Derbyshire had been selected for an assistant port director in California, Lynn was going into an investigations job in Texas and Sam was going to be the OIC in Bangkok, Thailand. We would all be leaving Guam within weeks and months of one another. This would be my last assignment under Sam Martin. The family back home was overjoyed that we would be returning even though I would be in Florida and they would all be in Oklahoma.

One of the nicest and surprising "Curve Balls" came to me on the Friday before we were to depart

Guam. Governor Carl Guiterres summoned me to his office and requested that I come in my dress uniform for my meeting with him. The governor's waiting room was filled to SRO capacity when I arrived, but I was escorted directly into his office. We had become friends during my tour on Guam, but we had never met in the manner in which we were meeting on this day. After a cup of coffee and some small talk, the governor opened his office door and invited the Press Corps and news media people into the office. Through a proclamation from the Governor and a unanimous vote of the Guam Senate, I was being awarded the Ancient Order of the Chamorri and becoming a full-fledged citizen Of Guam. During both my Air Force and INS Careers, I had received ribbons and other honors, but this one had me speechless. I have the certificate on my office wall at the house and it has hung on every office wall I have ever had since it was awarded to me. Barbara and I both still have very good friends on Guam with whom we communicate through cards, letters and our computers. I have going back to Guam on my bucket list and will visit there again one day. Haifa Dai to all of my good friends and brothers and sisters in Guam until we meet again.

Chapter 22
Miami 1996 to 2001

Barbara, Ron, Rob and I arrived in Florida in early April of 1996.   We met with our realtors Pam and Summer.   We had been communicating with them over the past couple of months and they were ready to show and sell us our new house in Florida.   They made arrangements for temporary housing that was beautiful and exceeded our expectations.   We got settled into our temporary quarters and began looking for a house the very next day.   We could have purchased any of the houses that they showed us, as they had done their homework.   Every house they showed us met all of the specifications that we had told them we were looking for.

Barbara has this t-shirt that reads: I Breath; Therefore I shop.   She really loves to shop and lives up to the saying on her t-shirt.   I hope that you are sitting down while you are reading this page, for I ended up buying Barbara a house just across the highway from the largest mall in Florida. The mall is about the size of Delaware.   The good thing for me was that it only took two trips to Sawgrass Mills Mall for the novelty to wear off.   There were a million other places to shop in the area that were less congested. The cruise lines and the airports brought busloads of foreign visitors to the mall and it was a real nightmare getting around in there some days when the ships were in port.

The Miami district, like Guam, was going through some changes in management due to unusual circumstances. When we arrived, the district had a Temporary District Director (DD), Temporary Assistant

DD, Temporary Port Director and Temporary ADD for inspections. All of the people in upper management positions were held by people on detail. Most of these people would eventually apply for and get accepted for their positions permanently.

Barbara and I rode together for the first few months as I was assigned to a really good day shift. I would drop Barbara off at the district office, go to work at the airport and then pick her up after work. We were able to spend quite a lot of time together and did a lot of Florida sightseeing on the weekends. We both fell in love with the Sunshine State and hope to move there permanently one day. We actually ended up liking Florida much more than California. Florida had less expensive housing, no state tax, plenty of sunshine and palm trees.

My natural mother and her husband Don had retired and owned a home in Naples, Florida and we visited them as often as our schedules allowed. I really got to know my mom and we became very close as a result of those visits. I never asked anything about why she and my dad had divorced and it never came up in any of our conversations. We were together now and that's all that mattered at the time. Don and one of his friends had purchased a really nice pontoon boat and they took us out on it a time or two.

My next "Curve Ball" came on Veteran's Day, November 11, 1997. Don called to tell us that my mother had passed away. She had been ill for years with emphysema and was on oxygen 24 hours a day, seven days a week. I will always be grateful for the time we had together in 1996 and 1997. I firmly believe that my life's "Guiding Forces" had a hand in my being assigned to Miami at that time in my career. My mom died knowing that I loved her very much and I think that gave her some piece of mind.

My next "Curve Ball" came when a new port director was selected and she turned out to be less than what I expected in a supervisor. Dora Jean had a management style that was 360 degrees from mine. She disliked me and the other Associate Port Director from the very start. I had always looked forward to going to work, but now dreaded every day that I had to go there under her supervision. She had a bullwhip hanging from her wall that she was quite proud of and it was the very first thing you saw when you entered her office. It was so offensive, that some of the troops filed a grievance through their union to have it removed. Dora had me and the other Associate Port Director transferred to the district office shortly after her first annual appraisal of us. I was assigned to locate and get leases for four fingerprint offices where applicants would be processed under an INS special program. There was a deadline for locating and securing the sites, training the staff and processing applicants. I was the lead officer, and worked with two other officers from the Miami district. We were able to beat the established deadline and through our efforts, the Miami district was the first district to process 1,000, 10,000 and 100,000 applicants. Attorney General Janet Reno would visit and dedicate one of these offices. She was more than generous with her praise for our efforts in handling this project. Bob Wallis the DD and Jack Bulger the ADD gave me an outstanding annual appraisal and a very nice cash bonus to accompany it. I had made a good impression on Mr. Bulger and he next assigned me to develop and teach a customer service program for the Miami district. At that time, we were getting an unusually large number of complaints relating to bad customer service on the part of the Miami employees. Mr. Bulger provided me with a really great office with plenty of room to work. He just turned me loose to work on the program. I ended up developing and writing lesson plans for a two day (16 hour) customer service/cultural awareness program that I would teach over the next two years. I taught this program to all assigned personnel at the district office, airport, Khrome Detention Center and all Miami satellite stations to include both Freeport and Nassau in the Bahamas. I presented this program to over 1,700 INS employees in Florida and traveled all over the state and the islands of the Bahamas.

Mr. Bulger presented me with several awards and cash bonuses at rating time over this period. The award I was most proud of was an award he called "Thinking Out of the Box". It came with a trophy to match the award. In January of 2001, I traveled to Baltimore and presented the two day program to their entire staff including their DD and ADD. I will always be most grateful and hold a special place in my heart for Mr. Bulger for what he did to resurrect my career and give me back my sense of pride.

Dora Jean was eventually transferred and replaced by Walter H. Lee Jr. as the port director at Miami International Airport. Walter would eventually have me transferred back to MIA where I truly belonged. Walter was and is a no-nonsense, straight forward supervisor with the greatest sense of fairness of anyone I have ever worked for. He surrounded himself with good people, gave them a sense of direction and then allowed them the freedom to do their jobs. He ran a great operation in Miami and was and is very well liked and respected throughout the service.

We received a horrendous "Curve Ball" when our son Rob called to tell us that he was at the doctor with Nana (Barb's mom) and that the doctor had told him that Nana had pancreatic cancer. The doctor told him that the cancer had advanced to the point where there was nothing they could do for her. We went to see Mr. Bulger to try to make arrangements for Barbara to take a long-term leave without pay so that she might go to Oklahoma to be with her mom. Jack Bulger got on the phone and before we knew it, Barbara had been detailed to the Oklahoma City Office where she would be able to work and still be with her mom. We will never be able to put into words the appreciation and love with have for Jack Bulger as a supervisor and as a man. Jack always talked about INS as a family and he treated all of his employees like they were, in fact, members of his extended family. There has got to be a special place for people like him.

I drove Barbara to Oklahoma in our new van and had made arrangements for two weeks leave so that I might spend time with the woman I called Mom. Mom wanted to go to Indiana to personally tell the family about her illness and the fact that the doctor had only given her six months to live. We put the seats down, inserted a mattress and made the trip to Indiana just fine. One of mom's final requests to me was that I take her to the casino in Michigan so that she could gamble one more time. When she and dad lived in California, they were always going to Las Vegas and she really liked her slot machines. I took her, she gambled and we all had a great time. No one knows for certain how they might act if they were given the kind of news that mom got from her doctor, but my only hope is that I would be able to handle it with the grace and dignity that mom did. When I left Oklahoma, I bought an open-ended roundtrip ticket and would do so every time I visited. Barbara called me on October 17th and told me to come home now. She told me that mom had been asking when I was coming and it was as if she knew the end was near. Mom died the day after I arrived on October 19, 2000. She died while we held hands and listened to her favorite Elvis Pressley CD. It is ironic that the song that was playing when she took her final breath was *Amazing Grace* and I felt that was the most fitting way this wonderful and gentle woman should pass away.

Barbara's Aunt Jo, Uncle Paul and Uncle Chester traveled from Indiana to be there for mom's services. Barb's cousin Gene, who mom called Genie, came all the way from Florida to say good-bye to his favorite aunt. Father Jim held a really beautiful service for mom and gave me the opportunity to speak. Saying good-bye to mom was hands down the most difficult thing I have ever done or hope to do. I have said this before, but we have a picture of mom and dad that has hung in every living room we have ever had or will have and I still talk to both of them on occasion.

We were lucky to have them as parents. I will always be grateful for the way they treated me from the moment I said "I Do" to Barbara until they passed away. I still get really upset when I hear some ungrateful guy tell a mother-in-law joke. Barbara's mom had given her pride and joy Buick Century to Barbara and she drove it back to Florida while I drove her van. We went back to work almost immediately and Barbara adjusted very well.

We had been in Miami since 1996 and I was starting to get an itch on the bottom of my feet. I began applying for jobs around the service and was particularly interested in a position in the Bahamas. I made mention to Mr. Bulger one day in passing how much I was interested in going there and low and behold, I was selected. We would be leaving the Miami district.

Chapter 23
My Bahama Mama

I was selected for the position of assistant port director in February of 2001 for Nassau in the Bahamas. Barbara and I would be making plans to move once again. Barbara decided to ship her mom's car to Nassau. She sold her van to Kari and Mike for a really good below book price. I purchased a Chrysler Lebaron convertible that I would drive. Thanks once again to Jack Bulger, Barbara was also going to have a position in the airport in Nassau. She would have to take a demotion in order to continue working, but it didn't seem to matter to her. Barbara has always supported me and the family and has never hesitated to make sacrifices for all of us. My new boss was Jim Carbonneau, who I knew, liked and respected. I was really excited about returning to an island.

Barbara had gone through all four years of high school in Bermuda and we had done our tour on Guam. We were both developing a fondness for island living and were anxiously awaiting our transfer. Jim was able to secure a house for us prior to our arrival. Barbara and I went over for a day to see it. We were met by Jim and his wife Karen when we arrived. Karen took us to see the house, to lunch at what became one of our favorite places to eat and gave us the most wonderful tour of the island. Karen was and is one of the most gracious ladies that you would ever want to meet and befriend. She also decorates for Christmas like no one you will ever see. The house that Jim had secured for us was fantastic. It even had a really nice pool, avocado trees, banana trees and a great yard for entertaining. We had a lot of really great parties in that house.

We arrived in Nassau on a Friday afternoon and once again Jim had done something very special for us. Our house was not ready and our things had not arrived, therefore, we would be spending a couple of weeks in temporary housing. Jim arranged for us to stay in an area called Sandy Port. It was one of the very nicest areas on the island, just off one of the main roads and very near the airport. I know that this may sound silly, but you can actually get lost on an island until you know your way around. With that in mind, Barbara and I spent the weekend just driving around and seeing where things were. Jim had made arrangements for me to use one of the airport vehicles until our cars arrived. The Bahamas have some of the most beautiful and inviting waters in all of the Caribbean and I froze my tushy off when I went for a swim that weekend. The water in the Bahamas is a little chilly, actually cold, from October through mid-April and it was just a little early then. Barbara and I were amazed at all of the beautiful flowers that were in bloom and the palm trees that seemed to touch the sky. When you see all of this beauty, you come to realize that Mother Nature had to have a helping hand. It is so beautiful.

Barbara and I both started working on the Monday after we arrived. Since Nassau was under the supervision of the Miami district, all of our processing had been done before we left there. All we had to do that first day was go to the American Embassy and clear there. Barbara was going to be Jim's secretary and Jack of all trades during our assignment there. She did just about everything for Jim and to this day sings his praises as one of the best bosses she has ever had. We had sold our house in Florida, paid off most of our other bills and would live quite comfortably in the Bahamas. The American Embassy provided housing and paid all utilities at no cost to us. All we had to pay was our phone bill and TV cable.

I was assigned as one of two assistant port directors under Jim Carbonneau and my counterpart was a guy by the name of Jim Zenny. Jim Zenny and his family had orders and would be rotating back to Florida in the near future. I worked Monday through Thursday that first week with Friday and Saturday as my days off. Jim Carbonneau liked to rotate his APD's for every other Sunday, so I would be working the early shift the next coming Sunday. At that time, the port had INS inspectors, customs inspectors and agricultural inspectors. All of these were separate entities. I would only be supervising the INS officers who were on duty. During this first shift, I met and talked with the customs and agriculture supervisors and got to know them a little. It turned out that the agriculture supervisor was Ingrid Zenny the wife of my co-worker. She was excited and talked about their upcoming move back to Florida. She told me that she was a registered nurse and that she had been hired for a really great nursing position. She and Jim had two children. They seemed so happy and were looking forward to going home. Jim Zenny received a devastating "Curve Ball" at 5am the next morning when Ingrid Zenny was killed in an automobile accident on her way to work. It appeared that she was in a bit of a hurry and she didn't quite navigate a sharp curve in the road. She hit a tree and her car flipped over. She was not wearing her seat belt and was thrown from and pinned under her car. We were all at work when the news started drifting in about the accident and I was dumbfounded by the news. I immediately thought back to the previous afternoon and recalled how excited Ingrid had been about their move and now she was gone. I was almost 60 years old at the time and remember thinking how quickly the best laid plans of life can be altered by fate. Jim Zenny was off that day and was home getting the kids ready for school when he got the call. He had been requested by the Bahamian Police to come to the scene of the accident and identify the body of his wife. If I live to be one hundred, I would never want to feel what Jim Zenny must have been feeling when he made that drive to the scene of his wife's death. Barbara would drive by the accident scene on her way to work at 7:30. She saw the accident scene. She was a mess when she arrived at the airport. My wife is the kindest, sweetest and most caring person I know and I am certain that this is something that will stay in her memory forever.

A funeral service for Ingrid was held a few days later at St. Paul's Catholic Church in Lyford Key. Barbara attended the service along with the people from the airport and the American Embassy. We allowed all who we could spare to go to this service. Some of the inspectors also set up a small memorial in the airport. It was inspiring to see inspectors, passengers and airline personnel stopping to pay their last respects to this woman that some of them did not even know. It restored my faith in my fellow man.

Jim Carbonneau made one of the most heartwarming gestures I have ever seen, when he allowed the staff to go out to the cargo area and say the final good-bye's to Mrs. Zenny. I think that it was something that gave the troops some closure. I will always respect Jim for that. The airport authority had placed the coffin just a few feet from our back door. We all had our minute or so to say our final good-bye. I am not too proud or too macho to tell you that I cried when I said my final farewell to this woman, wife and mother.   Jim and the children left for Florida where they would be surrounded by family.

During this time we were getting in a lot of new inspectors from all over the country.   I was really lucky and most of these new officers would be assigned to me.   I ended up the first line supervisor for Mark Spence, Paul (PAULIE) Schmidt, Gilbert and Jackie Gauthier, Robert Leva and several others.   The officers who were assigned to me were of the same mind set as me.   On occasion, Jim referred to them as My Enforcement Bunch.   Paul and Mark, in particular, sent more good cases to secondary than anyone else in Nassau.   They followed the letter of the law and were thorough in both primary and secondary inspections.   With Jim Zenny being gone, Jim Carbonneau assigned some of the journeymen officers to his position on 90 day rotations.   It was a busy and hectic time for us all.

One of the best things about being stationed in a place like Nassau is that you get to see family and friends more often.   Every time I turned around, we were expecting visitors.   We have always welcomed visitors.   I really enjoyed when family and friends visited.   Mike and Kari visited us every chance they got and both Casey and Jessica stayed with us for extended periods.   Lee and Claudia Livingston and Gary, Kathy and Steven Sanders also came and spent vacations with us.   Again I thank Jim Carbonneau for arranging for my housing that accommodated all of them.

Barbara had fallen in love with St Paul's church after she had gone there for Ingrid's funeral service and we became members there shortly after that.   We made a lot of friends at St. Paul's, and I would eventually become the director of religious education for the church.   Our parish priest was Father Bob.   He became, not just our priest, but our very good friend. Father had a German Sheppard named Ziegfeld that was the biggest dog I had ever seen.   Ziggy was Father's constant companion, and followed him everywhere he went.   Ziggy even attended the evening mass on Saturday evening the whole time we were in the Bahamas.   Barbara was always cooking something for Father Bob or we would go by and get him some KFC, so Ziggy came to know that we were the good guys.   I always took Ziggy some sort of treat.   He got to the point that he would climb in my car and sniff around for his goodies.   When Barbara and I went to mass, Ziggy would come to where I was sitting and have me scratch behind his ears before mass started.   In addition to Father Bob, we made other friends who we still stay in touch with and visit every chance we get.   Mario Portundo and I are like brothers and he always has us out to lunch and gives us his car to drive when we visit there.   We always schedule our visits to the Bahamas to include Saturday evening mass so that we get the opportunity to see and visit with all of our friends there.

My generation grew up admiring our hero's and I have never quite outgrown my fascination with them. One of the very best experiences I had in Nassau was the opportunity to meet Secretary of State Colin Powell.   General Powell was my hero from the first Gulf War along with Stormin' Norman.   Secretary Powell had come to Nassau to sign some sort of treaty with the Bahamas and he took time to visit all of us at the airport during his visit.   He gave a short speech, opened the floor for questions and then mingled with the troops to chat and sign autographs.   When he approached me, I rendered my very best salute and said, "Good afternoon General."   He smiled, thanked me and returned my salute.   Barbara took a picture of the exchange of salutes and I got an autographed picture of Secretary Powell. Mrs. Powell came to me a few minutes later and thanked me for saluting the General. She told me that he was a soldier at heart and that he was pleased when people remembered that he was once a General.

In June of 2002, I was selected for the position of assistant port director for Seaport Operations in Houston, Texas and would be leaving the Bahamas. I learned the next day that I had been selected for this position by newly assigned Port Director Walter H. Lee Jr. It would be like going home. I was very excited to have the opportunity to work for Walter once again. He already had the district office working on finding a position for Barbara and she would have a job when we arrived. We were moving, once again, to a place we had never been before and the wife of my life took it in stride. I don't think that she had even finished unpacking from our move from Miami to Nassau and here I was relocating her again. The good part about all of this is that we have both gotten to see many places that we probably could not have afforded to otherwise. The other thing that amazes me is how very quickly Barbara has been able to turn our new houses into homes.

Chapter 24
Deep in the Heart of Houston

We flew into Houston on August 20, 2002 which was Barbara's birthday. We were met by Walter Lee and Phil Danely. Walter had arranged for a suite for us in a really great place that was exactly the same driving distance to both the airport and the district office where Barbara would be working. Walter and Phil helped us unload the car and get settled into the suite. He then drove us to a place where he had arranged to get us a rental car. In between all of this, he gave me my new badge and he made me feel like I was a member of the team. We had sold my car in Nassau and had shipped Barbara's mom's Buick along with our household items. It was mid-afternoon on a Friday and we would have the weekend to find our way around and to try to get familiar with the area.

I had been in telephone contact with Letty Alcazar who would be working for me at the seaport. She had hooked us up with a realtor. Our realtor would pick us up on Saturday morning and we would begin our search for a house. We were trying to get into an area that would be an easy driving distance for both of us. Barbara would be working in the north part of Houston and my office was in the south part of the city. Susan had really done her homework, and almost everything she showed us fit the bill. After having our own pool in Nassau, we both wanted a house with a pool. Susan showed us a number of very nice houses in the Humble, Texas area. We ended up purchasing a house at 6003 Caldicote Street in Humble. The house was empty, it had a pool and Barbara fell in love with the his and hers walk-in closets. It was a little bit further for me to drive, but it was all freeway once I got out of the housing area.

We also found a church that was near the house that had both Saturday and Sunday masses. We became members and attended it the whole time we lived in Houston. Our first Houston "Curve Ball" came on the day of closing. It would cause us some minor problems over the first couple of months. Walter was in desperate need for one of his assistant port director's to go to headquarters for some serious computer training and I volunteered when he couldn't get anyone else to go. I would be in Washington and Barbara would go to the closing along with my power of attorney that was suggested by the realtor and title company. There was some glitch in the closing that day. Barbara and I would end up closing a few weeks later.   This would become the house we would remember for its tough time closing" and its tough time selling, but that will all come later. Our street turned out to be a good one. We had excellent neighbors on both sides of us and across the street. It was a nice quiet area, with low traffic flow and very few children. The only problem we had was the gigantic pine tree that was right in the middle of the front yard. I spent a lot of time raking up very long pine needles and picking up pinecones the size of horse doo-doo, and that's what I called them. You know from reading this book that I have always had a force looking after me and this would be no exception. One night we had a terrible storm. The top 10 to 15 feet of that tree was hit by lightning and posed a threat to the roof of the house. We applied for and received permission from the home owners association to have it taken down for the safety of our house, cars and us. I don't know how many times I have raved about what a great wife Barbara was, but in Houston she out did herself. I needed a car, as I had sold mine when we left Nassau. We went to Car Max and Barbara allowed me to buy an Elvis gold Cadillac that was the nicest car I had ever owned. I found out that God must drive a Cadillac and it came to me as the result of some bad Houston weather. Our garage has always been at least half full of boxes and cartons from all of our moves and my car would always be the one to get parked outside on the driveway. One night we had a horrendous hail storm that lasted for over 15 minutes straight. I just knew that my Elvis gold Cadillac was going to look like a waffle and that all of my windows would be broken or cracked. When the sun came up the next morning, I went out to access the damages to me car before calling our insurance company.   We had over $12,000.00 in damages to our roof, but there was not one single mark or scratch or anything at all wrong with my Cadillac. It was then and there that I decided that God must drive one too and didn't allow mine to get hurt.

The seaport turned out to be one of my very best assignments. Letty and the staff worked very hard and I could always count on them to go the extra mile for me. Letty was the first line supervisor over all of the seaport staff. She did such a great job that sometimes I felt like I was just a figure head and she really ran the place. Her favorite saying was that everything was just peachy keen and I tagged her with that as a nickname. I was at a Cracker Barrel Restaurant and they had an insert in their menu for a dessert item called the Peachy Keen. I took it and brought it back for Letty. We have both have retired since our days together in Houston, but we still keep in touch. Letty is one of the good guys. Between her and Walter Lee looking after me, I can honestly say this job ranked at the top of my working career list.

My next "Curve Ball" came when two of my guys called in sick about fifteen minutes before they were to go and inspect a large cruise ship. I did not have time to get replacements, so Letty and I took their places for the inspection. This was not the first ship I had ever inspected, so off we all went in the old government van down to the ship. The game plan was for me to go on board and assist with the inspection of the U.S. citizens, which was the easiest part of the inspection and involved the most number of passengers. None of this was new to me, as I was always doing some type of inspection somewhere in the port. I will always remember the first ship I boarded after my arrival in Houston and how astonished the Captain and crew were to be inspected by what they referred to as the big boss. It was not normal for someone of my rank and position to go on board and inspect. Every time I did it, I got the same kind of stunned look from the crew. Letty also told me that my predecessor rarely left his office and never inspected ships. My philosophy has always been that I would not ask or order a person to do something that I would not do myself and to demonstrate that every once in a while. While I was inspecting the U.S. citizens, a lady from Corsicana, Texas presented me with her paperwork for inspection. I remembered that this was where Gary Sanders, my old Air Force friend, was from. I asked the lady if she might know him or know if he still lived there. As it turned out, she and Gary's address block together in the same bank back in Corsicana. I can't tell you how many times while driving through there that I would say to Barbara, "I wonder if Gary Sanders still lives here?"

I gave the lady my card and asked if she would try

to get it to him. Three days later Gary called and we made arrangements to meet him in Corsicana the next weekend. This would be the first time we would have seen each other in over 40 years. Both Barbara and I were excited about the reunion. Gary, Kathy, Barbara and I are all still good friends today. We have gone on vacations and cruises together. We try to make it a point to get together at least once a month if it's just for lunch or dinner. The older you get, the fewer old friends you seem to have.

INS received what we perceived to be a "Curve Ball" on March 3, 2003 when the Department of Homeland Security was formed. INS, Customs, Agriculture, The Border patrol and the Coast Guard would all come under U.S. Customs and Border Protection (CBP). INS, Customs and Agriculture were all put in the same uniform that was very much like the old customs' uniforms. Even our badges and credentials were changed. The early days of this merger were a nightmare. None of us was feeling really good about all of the changes. We had all developed our former agencies mentality and identity and it felt like all of that was being taken away. You know, of course, that all of these changes came about as a result of 9/11. It would turn out alright once every officer accepted and got on board with the changes. The one gigantic, positive in all of this, was that most of the GS levels were going to be raised and there were going to be more job opportunities in more locations in the future. Shortly after the merger, I was reassigned to Houston International Airport as one of its chief inspectors. CBP had even changed our job titles. Now instead of being an assistant port director, I was going to be a chief. It took me a long time to get accustomed to people calling me chief. Every once in a while, one of the troops would have to tap me on the arm to get my attention. Nothing had changed in our pay grade or in the authority that we had, but I just never quite got the hang of being called chief.

In May of 2003, I was contacted by J.T. Lawson from my old DFW days. He was requesting that I come to his duty station to teach my two day customer service program. After several phone calls, it was determined that I would go on a detail to Texas and Oklahoma to provide this program for the Dallas district. I would also end up teaching it to the Houston CBP staff when I returned from that detail.

I spent the remainder of my time in Houston alternating between the airport and seaport as I was needed. In the summer of 2004, I began to apply for positions all over the world. As I said, grade levels were being raised and more positions in more locations had opened up due to the merging of the agencies. I applied for several positions in Canada, Ireland, Aruba, the Virgin Islands and in the Bahamas. Walter Lee called me at home one evening to tell me that he had just gotten off the phone after talking to a man from headquarters. He said that they had called about my applications and wanted to know if he felt that I would be qualified for a port director position. He said that he had spoken with a guy named Joe, but couldn't remember his last name. After Walter's call, I went on a pins and needles status and stayed there for some time. In mid-August, just before Barbara's birthday, I received a call from Joe O'Gorman from headquarters. He told me that I had been selected for the position of Area Port Director over all of the islands of the Bahamas. I received this call in my office at the Houston Seaport and was instructed NOT to say anything to anybody except for my wife until I received official notification from human resources. I told Joe that I would not say anything to anyone, but my wife, in accordance with his instructions. My entire staff was in my doorway as they knew that I had put in for jobs and that this call was from headquarters, but I said nothing to them. I called Barbara, and as I remember it I asked, "Do you want to be my Bahama Mama?"

My question caught her completely off guard, but my staff went crazy with my good news. I would be going back to Nassau as the Area Port Director and the very first ever GS-14.

My next "Curve Ball" came when I received my official notification and was informed that because of the position, Barbara would not be able to work in Nassau. It was some mumbo-jumbo about spouses not being allowed to have their life's partners" in their chain of command.

I really wanted this position and knew it would take some fancy footwork" on my part to get it. Barbara was of an age and at the point in her INS career where she could retire with full benefits and that is exactly what she did for me. She was really not ready to retire, but knowing how much this job meant to me, she made another sacrifice. As her reward, which she always refers to as a bribe, I sold my Elis gold Caddy, traded in my Chevy pick-up truck and bought her an Inferno Red Chrysler Convertible. We even put the title in just her name and it became her 2004 birthday present. I like to call it her reward for her 26 years with INS or her birthday present, but to this day she still calls it a bribe. I ended up with the Buick and Barbara had a really beautiful red convertible in which she would drive around the island.

Barbara was able to continue working in the Houston District Office almost until the time we left. I rotated between the airport and seaport. This would turn out to be my final assignment under Walter Lee and I will always be grateful to him for all he did for me throughout my INS and CBP careers.   I still consider and have him as one of my friends and we communicate when we can.

Me in My Houston Office

Chapter 25
Back To Nassau

I reported to Nassau in early February of 2005, after a short visit to Washington for some training with Glen Ross and Angel McKinney. Barbara and I received a minor "Curve Ball" on the day we arrived in Nassau when no one was there to meet us and assist with our things. We were really loaded down with baggage and our cat in her portable kennel. My new secretary, Jill, spotted us at about the half-way point and assisted us over to my new office.

The embassy housing representative had made arrangements with Jill to meet us at our new house, so she loaded up the cat, our baggage, some welcoming kits and us and took off for the house. The house was partially furnished and we would do fine until our things arrived from Houston. We went over the furniture inventory and general condition of the house with Mr. Burke. We signed all of the necessary forms for occupancy. Mr. Burke then took us to a car rental and we rented a car until our own cars would arrive. After all of the moves we had made throughout our careers, we were accustomed to living out of cartons, boxes and suitcases, so we were all set.

Jill turned out to be one of the very best and most efficient people I have ever worked with. She really kept me focused and on track in my early days in Nassau. Jill would, however, deliver me my next "Curve Ball" when she informed me that Mrs. Sava, my new boss, had scheduled a meeting with all port directors for the last week in February in Toronto,

Canada. When I departed Nassau it was a balmy 85 degrees, and when I arrived in Canada it was a balmy -4 degrees. I spent the next two days and three nights freezing my butt off. I remember, at the time, I did not own any real winter clothing as all of my things were being shipped. Paul Schmidt let me borrow his INS leather jacket. Paul does not know it, but he probably saved me from freezing to death. Toronto was beautiful and the airport was a first class operation, but we all requested that our next meeting be in a warmer climate. Jennifer complied and our next meeting was in Arlington, Virginia.

While I was port director in Nassau, I had the habit of visiting the airport on either Saturday or Sunday to see how things were going and let the staff know I was available. I remember going on one such visit on Barbara's birthday and ending up staying there for over three hours. Our original game plan for that day was to stop by the airport, visit with some friends and then just drive around the island with the top down. When we arrived at the airport, they were jam packed and really backed out the doors with passengers. I had Barbara go to my office and I took over directing passengers to and through the inspection process. After the first thirty minutes, Barbara came out of my office, looked around the area and gave me THE LOOK. I noticed that she would come out about every 15 minutes after her first visit and she would go through the same ritual ending with The LOOK. On one occasion when she went back to my office, I instructed the staff, the passengers and the airport personnel to all shout "Happy Birthday Barbara" the next time she appeared in the doorway. They did a great job of wishing her a Happy Birthday and she almost forgave me for tying up her special day.
When we had departed Houston, we put our house at

6003 Caldicote on the market and continued to make our house payments. Real estate was really slow at the time and we did not have any prospects or contracts. Our government property managers suggested that we allow them to rent the property as rentals were in high demand. They promised that they would do background checks and interview applicants so that we would get the very best renters possible. They also stated that they would and could rent it for more than our house payment. What a deal!

I paid an official visit to Freeport on August 24, 2005 to meet the staff there and to present some awards. I had made arrangements to stay in Freeport for two days and return to Nassau on August 26th to celebrate my birthday. Hurricane Katrina hit Freeport as a Category 1"storm on the night of August 25th. I ended up stranded in Freeport for my birthday. Barbara has always said that it was my punishment for the three hours I made her stay at the airport on her birthday.

Our property manager called us a few days after Katrina hit New Orleans and requested our permission to rent our house to a family whose home was destroyed. The property manager told me that she had done all of the check and that they were a very nice family of four. They were even willing to put down security deposits and promised to take good care of the house. As it turned out, they were the best tenants we have ever had. They treated the house as if it was their own. With the house rented and occupied, Barbara and I could relax a little knowing that real people were now looking after our house.

My management team in Nassau was fantastic and very supportive. I will always be grateful for the outstanding manner in which they ran the port for me.

My two chief inspectors, Len Young and LaFonda Burke, alternated as Acting PD anytime I was called away. They always did very well. In addition, they were the first line supervisors for the SII's and the second line supervisors for all of the troops. Len was former INS and LaFonda was former Customs, so I had the very best in experience in both major areas of the CBP inspections process. Greg Moore, Carole Bell and Julia Bradshaw were three of the sharpest, hardworking and dedicated officers I have ever worked with and they managed first line supervision for me.

I also came to meet, know and befriend noted people on my second tour in Nassau, as I had on my first tour. During this tour, I met Jeb Bush the Governor of Florida, Condi Rice the Secretary of State and movie actor Sean Connery who was the original James Bond 007. I also worked closely with the U.S. Ambassador and his staff at the American Embassy. Ambassador John Rood was great to work with and for. He had more energy than a room full of kindergartners. He was on the go 24/7, but always made time to make himself available to all departments. I held a monthly staff meeting at the airport to bring my guys up to date and present awards.

The Ambassador came and spoke at every one of these meetings, helped me pass out awards, posed for photos and sat down to lunch with us. My entire staff really like, respected and appreciated Ambassador Rood. He was from Jacksonville, Florida and was a big Jaguars fan. He and I went round and round during football season. I remember one time when the owner of the Jaguars came to Nassau to visit the Ambassador, and John called me to make arrangements to show his visitor around the airport.

The airport was undergoing some remodeling and upgrading at the time and John wanted to show the construction site to his visitor.   Knowing that his visitor was the owner of the Jacksonville Jaguars, I made the Ambassador wear my Pittsburgh Steelers hard hat in the construction area. John reluctantly donned the hard hat and his visitor teased him all through the tour.   John Rood was a good sport. We laughed about that incident for a long time to come.

My next "Curve ball" came in mid-July of 2006, when our property manager called to let us know that our renters were moving back to New Orleans in August.   Barbara and I made arrangements to travel back to Houston to check on the house and meet with the property managers.   Barbara had also made an appointment for me with her cardiologist when my administrative assistant Leticia Robinson ratted me out to Barbara.   Leticia had come into my office one morning when I was having some really bad chest pains.   According to Leticia, I was an awful shade of gray.   I have always had a very high pain tolerance level and told Leticia not to worry about it or say anything to anybody.   She said okay and went directly to her office and called Barbara.   I have come to realize that Leticia probably saved my life with that call.   She will always be one of mine and Barbara's favorite people on the planet.

After checking out the house and discovering it was okay, we decided to put it back on the market since I was going to be in the Bahamas for at least three more years.   I had an appointment with Barbara's cardiologist on Wednesday, August the 1st. That one visit would change my whole life as I knew it.   Dr. Wei admitted me to the hospital for a cardiac cauterization after he performed some routine tests. The cauterization was scheduled for Friday morning on

August 3, 2006. It would be performed by a Dr. Gammon. Dr. Gammon and I had the opportunity to talk prior to the procedure and I told him about my cardiology experience with the Air Force. I told him that I was completely familiar with the procedure and understood what would be happening during it. Dr. Gammon had his technicians position me on the table, so that I could watch what was going on during the procedure. Once the catheters are in place, a dye is injected and is supposed to travel through the arteries of the heart to tell the doctor the location and severity of the heart disease. I remember watching as the dye was injected and it not going anywhere and me saying very loudly, "OH SHIT" about the trouble I knew I was in with my heart. After the procedure, while I was still lying on the table, Dr. Gammon went over the results with Barbara. I remember Dr. Gammon saying, "You see this right here Barbara?"

Barbara said, "Yes."

Dr. Gammon then said to Barbara, "We call this the widow maker."

I could hear the shakiness in Barbara's voice as she responded. He did this two more times in describing what he was showing her. It was at this point that I spoke up with, "Hey, guys I am wide awake here and have heard all that you said."

The results of the procedure showed that I had three major blockages in my arteries and an abdominal aortic aneurism that would require two major surgeries over the next couple of months.

The by-pass surgery went well thanks to the capable hands of the cardiovascular folks in Houston. I was well on my way to recovery. My game plan was to take a 30 day convalescent leave and then return to full duty status in Nassau. Barbara returned to Nassau on August 17, 2006 and Rob came to the

house in Houston to look after and care for old dad.
We stayed in the house in Houston, so we did have a
roof over our heads.   I still don't know how it
happens, but things always seem to fall into place for
me at the times when I need them the most.

The granddaddy of all "Curve Balls" was delivered
to me on August 20, 2006 in the form of a phone call
from a Dr. Green from the Medical Unit of the
Department of State. The good, the bad and the ugly
have all happened to me on Barbara's birthday. This
was going to be another one of those ugly occasions.
I had carried my government cell phone with me from
Nassau, so that I might keep in touch with Len Young
whom I had placed in charge during the time I would
be off the island. This Dr. Green called me on that
line which meant it was official business. I was sitting
in my doctor's office awaiting my two week post-op
checkup when I got this call. Dr. Green informed me
that, after reviewing my medical records and the
reports from my surgeons, he was cancelling my
overseas medical clearance. He was telling me that I
would not be medically cleared to go back to Nassau.

Suddenly, with just one phone call, my life as I
knew it, would be drastically changed. Dr. Green told
me that he had already contacted my agency with his
decision and that I would need to contact them for
further instructions. I was feeling great physically,
but after his call, I felt like I had been kicked in the
stomach by a very angry elephant. I had a difficult
time trying to recall a time in my life when I hurt as
bad as I did at that moment. I was a dedicated and
hardworking officer who truly loved his job. I saw it
coming to an end with this phone call.

When I returned to the house, I called Jennifer
Sava and asked what my options would be under my
medical circumstances. Jennifer was sympathetic to

my condition, as her own father had undergone the same type of surgery. She told me that my two options were to either retire or accept a transfer to my home of record. Houston was considered my home of record, as that is where I was officially assigned prior to my transfer to the Bahamas. She informed me that she would assign Len Young to temporary duty as the Area Port Director and for me not to worry about anything except getting well. I decided that I was not ready to retire and requested re-assignment to Houston. My next call was to Barbara to break the news to her.

Barbara, like always, stepped up to the plate and hit a homerun or should I say a "Run Home". This was the worst birthday present ever delivered, but before we got off the phone she had already had me feeling better. Barbara would end up selling the Buick in Nassau, so at least a part of me was able to remain in the Bahamas. It was a really nice car and we had taken really good care of it. Barbara ended up selling it to a Bahamas Customs Officer before she left Nassau. Barbara also held several garage sales and was able to downsize what we would be sending home. Barbara told me that my staff from the airport was very sympathetic and all helped her when she most needed them. We would end up owing a lot to Rick and Ester James and John and Song Dietrich for all of the help and support that they provided. Rick, who is a computer genius, went so far as to color code and label all of my computer connections so that I would not have any problems re-connecting them. Barbara also received help and support from all of our friends from St. Paul's Church. Pat Breen and Barbara would go to the casino every day for their free money spins and they really became close friends over this period of time. We make it a point to stay in touch with them and visit when we can.

Due to the fact that Barbara sold the Buick, we determined that I would need to buy a car for work. When I was able to drive again, Rob drove me out to my favorite CarMax in search of a car for work. You guessed it! I ended up with my second Cadillac. Before I went to CarMax, I had gotten pre-approved for the money to buy a new car and in less than one hour I drove off the lot in my new car. Rob was a little homesick for Oklahoma, so he decided to go back home once I had my car and could take care of myself. To this day, I am convinced that I owe a great deal of my speedy recovery to Rob and his Black Lab Sheena. They took really good care of me and made certain that I got out of bed and did my exercises. Sheena watched over me as though I were one of her puppies that wasn't feeling well. I always make certain to take her some treats when we go to visit the boys in Oklahoma. Sheena always checks the places on my legs when the stitches were. I think she does that to make certain that they have healed.

While Barbara was getting things arranged in Nassau, I had our storage items delivered to the house, bought some new items and had the whole downstairs re-modeled. Rob and I painted and we had a company lay down laminate in the living areas and ceramic tile in the kitchen, laundry room and bathroom. When Barbara would finally arrive, it would be like walking into a new place. It would take Barbara a few really frustrating months, however, before she would come home to Houston. At one point in the process, someone from the American Embassy suggested that Barbara initiate a power of attorney to allow them to take care of our things. We decided that Barbara would stay, watch over our things and make all of the arrangements and decisions. We can only imagine what may have come up missing or stolen had we done as suggested. Barbara and the cat arrived in Houston in October and we resumed our life with CBP Houston.

Me in My Nassau Office

(Woody), informed me that I would be
working in the port office interviewing and taking
statements from officers who had complaints filed
against them. I had worn a badge, carried a gun and
enforced INS law since my days in Atlanta. Now it
appeared that I was being put out to pasture so to
speak. I think that part of this assignment was
concern about my health, as I still looked a little puny
at the time. This was in mid-September and I still
had to undergo the repair of the aneurism in October.
I also learned that Woody would be leaving and was
being replaced by a good friend of mine. I figured
that after my second surgery I would be able to return
to full duty and that Terry Estelle would give me an

assignment in keeping with my skills and experience. I had the aneurism repair in mid-October and my doctor placed me on a thirty day convalescent leave to give me time to properly heal.

The surgery procedure went very well, but the after affects are still with me today. When performing this type of surgery, the surgeon makes an incision on both sides of the groin and then inserts catheters into those openings to do the procedure. I had an extremely difficult time walking after the surgery and was not able to stand for long periods of time. It was even difficult to find a good sitting or lying position. I experienced a great deal of pain at the incision sites, in my legs and in my hips. I went back to work after my first thirty day leave, but only lasted one week before I was back on leave. Due to the after effects of both surgeries, it appeared that when and if I could return to duty that it would be limited. I had enough sick leave available at the time to stay on sick leave with CBP until February or March of 2007, but I decided it was time to say so-long to that part of my life. I retired from CBP on December 31, 2006. I miss it even today and will always wish I had been able to stay on board longer. I look back over the twenty years I spent with INS and CBP and think about all of the wonderful places I was able to visit. I also think about the really terrific men and women with which I served. I realize that there are people who dread getting up in the morning and thank God that I was blessed with two careers that I became very good at and loved. Lee and Claudia are also retired from INS and we all get into the habit of boring people with our stories from our days with the agency.

Chapter 27
Mansfield, Texas

After I retired from CBP, Barbara and I had the time to do whatever our little hearts desired for probably the first time in our lives. What we both ended up wanting was something useful to do with all of the time we now had. We were both really too young to just sit around just being old retired people. I was getting that old itch on the bottoms of my feet.

In early 2007, we were traveling to Oklahoma City to visit our sons, to Fort Worth and to Corsicana to visit our old Air Force and CBP friends. When we went to visit the boys, it usually involved staying overnight, as it was a seven hour drive from Houston to Oklahoma City. We would visit Gary and Kathy in Corsicana and sometimes stayed over at their house. We did the same with Lee and Claudia and even spent New Year's Eve of 2006 with them. Lee and Claudia usually throw a New Year's Eve party. Claudia makes her chili. This stuff is to die for and I always end up making certain that Claudia does not have much in the way of leftovers. Due to the fact that we were spending a great deal of time in Oklahoma City, Lee and Claudia's in Fort Worth or Gary and Kathy's in Corsicana, we decided to look for a house in the Dallas/Fort Worth areas. I had been doing some research on my computer and the town of Mansfield seemed like the perfect place to look. It is located just off highway 287 which was the road we were taking when we visited everyone. This location was also about 200 miles closer to Atlanta which would come in handy when we visited our daughters and their families. We had driven this road so much over the past few months that I knew almost all of the exits and what amenities were offered at each. I still take this route when we visit the boys and Gary and Kathy. I will always be happy we selected this area. We were ready to move and ready to get serious about it.

We contacted our Texas realtor, Lee Livingston, and told him what we were looking for. He set out to find us a house in Mansfield. Lee had been and still is in the real estate business and I felt good throwing some business his way. Barbara and I made arrangements to go to Lee and Claudia's for the weekend. Lee was lining up houses for us to look at. We looked at several houses and selected and decided on the house we now live in at 1807 Lakes Edge Blvd. in Mansfield, Texas. It has a nice pool, four bedrooms and three full baths. It is only ten minutes from Lee and Claudia and less than one hour to Gary and Kathy's house. We are also able to, but don't for some reason, visit with our sons more often.

We put the house in Houston on the market. In May of 2007, we relocated to Mansfield, Texas. The house in Houston would remain vacant for several months and we would be making two house payments for a while. We really had a lot of stuff when we moved and were forced to use two storage units, our garage and attic to hold it all. Lee, Claudia and their two grandson's helped us to unload the U-Haul at the storage units and couldn't believe all of the stuff we had for just two people. When our furniture was delivered from Houston, we filled the house and the garage with more stuff and started to settle in the new place.

In June of 2007, Barbara and I went on our first cruise and we both got hooked on it. We sailed out of Galveston with Lee and Claudia. We had a great time on the Ecstasy of the Seas. Our next "Curve Ball" came during that cruise when Barbara went to see the ship's doctor with a simple case of diarrhea. She ended up in quarantine for the remainder of that voyage. She was told to stay in our stateroom and have all meals delivered to her. We didn't quite follow that command, but she didn't infect anyone else on board.

Fortunately, we only had one more port of call and one day at sea before we would return home. Lee and Claudia stayed on board for the next port of call. We played miniature golf and just hung out doing things around the ship. I never go anywhere without my camera and I took a less than flattering picture of Claudia that we still talk about these days. Barbara was fine, but did earn the nickname of Typhoid Annie for the remainder of the cruise and on the drive home. She took it like the good sport she is. Overall we really did have a great time and consider that cruise as the best we have ever gone on. I think that the company we were keeping was a big part of that.

We had a really great Thanksgiving that year when Kari and her family and Jessica and her boyfriend came for the holidays. We did all of the typical Thanksgiving things. We ate a lot of turkey and watched a lot of football. Barbara and Kari really put on an "Old Fashioned Feed" and it was wonderful to be surrounded by family. We closed out 2007 with Christmas with our sons in Oklahoma and New Year's Eve with Lee and Claudia. We also signed a long-term lease and would finally have some financial help in making the Houston house payment. We rented the house in Houston to a lady with two children and two very large cats that we knew nothing about. She would be in the house until February of 2009 when we would put the house back on the market. The lady with the two large cats left our house, yard and pool in a gigantic mess. It would end up costing us a bundle to get it back in shape for sale. The house in Houston was great when we wanted to buy it, but we had a terrible time on the selling end of it. We had put it on the market three different times and even tried "For Sale by Owner" to no avail. When we did sell, it was the easiest sale we ever made and the buyers gave us our asking price and paid cash. I don't think we will ever be that lucky again, or was it luck. I think that someone was watching over us.

There wouldn't be any cruising in 2008, but I would make two trips to Pittsburgh to visit family, get a really great job at the Fort Worth Zoo and get really hooked on Tequila. I made my first trip to Pittsburgh in the early spring and went only because Barbara made me go. She has always said that I was not built to be retired and I was really getting on her nerves. I made the trip up there in two days. It was really great to see the family again. I had not been home since a brief stay in 2005. I stayed with my Aunt Roma and Uncle George. It was like I had never been away. Aunt Roma made me peanut butter cookies. I always feel as much at home there as I do in my own home by the way they treat me.

When I returned from Pittsburgh, I began looking in the Classifieds for some sort of job to get me out of Barbara's hair. I applied for and was hired to work in Guest Relations at the Fort Worth Zoo. I stayed on there through the summer. It was a good job and how cool is it when you tell people that you work at the zoo.

As I mentioned earlier, I really got hooked on Tequila. My addiction to Tequila began on June 22, 2008 and it gets worse every day. Before you get the idea that I am some sort of falling down drunk, I had better explain that Tequila is my mixed shepherd dog that I adopted from the Ferris, Texas Animal Shelter.

The shelter had named her Nicki, but she didn't look like a Nicki and the name just didn't suit her. After we brought her home, in Barbara's car (in which she had several accidents) we went to Wal-Mart to pick up the necessary puppy supplies. As we were checking out, the clerk made the comment that someone had just gotten a new puppy and asked what we named the dog. I explained that we had not named her yet, but were open for suggestions. The cashier showed us her name tag and said, "What's wrong with my name?"

Her name was Tequila. Now, my new puppy had a new home and a new name all in one morning. She has been "My Tequila" ever since that day. When we see the cashier at Wal-Mart, she always asks how Tequila is.

I made my second trip to Pittsburgh the day after Labor Day and took Gary Sanders with me. Gary had never been to that part of the country and he had a ball. I don't care where you are from in this great country of ours, but people can usually tell that you are not from their neck of the woods the minute you speak. My family got a big kick from listening to Gary's Texas drawl. I spent three days acting as an interpreter. They were really confused the first time Gary used the phrase "Fixin' to" when he was going to call home. I explained that fixin' to was almost the same as "going to' and by the time we were fixin' to leave, they were all using it. The family always asks me how Gary is doing when I talk with them, as they all really liked having him. Gary also couldn't get over how close we were as a family, and still remarks about it these days.

In 2009, I would make one more trip to Pittsburgh, visit Orlando with Gary and Kathy and have two different jobs before the year was out. On both of my previous trips to Pittsburgh, the family all asked about Barbara, so we decided to take a trip to Pittsburgh to visit my family and to Indiana to visit with Barbara's family. It was a nice trip and we were able to see everyone in both families. We didn't know it at the time, but this would be the last time we would see Barbara's Aunt Jo. She was in a nursing home and the whole family came there on our last night for a pizza party. I took a picture of Barbara, her Aunt and all of the cousins that Barbara still has on her desk. It was probably the last picture taken of Aunt Jo.

We also took a trip to our time share in Orlando with Gary and Kathy during the summer. We did all of the Universal Studios and Disney things you do there. We had a great drive to and from and a real nice time in Florida. It had been a long time since Kathy had been there and Gary had never been, so it was a nice adventure for them both.

When summer ended, I began substitute teaching at all grade levels for our local school district. I was doing very well and working almost every day at several of the schools. In mid-September I was contacted by Kevin Lewis who was the program director for the Criminal Justice Program for Kaplan College in Fort Worth. Kevin wanted to interview me for a full-time instructor position at his campus due to my degrees and experience with the Department of Justice. Kevin is a retired Arlington, Texas police officer. He is one of the sharpest people I would ever work with and for. Kevin knows more about constitutional law than most attorneys I know and is one of the most dedicated peace officers on the planet. He was and is a credit to everyone who ever served. A few days after the interview, Kevin called and offered me a very well paying position which I readily accepted. Even though the majority of my work would be at night, I resigned my position with the local school district. I preferred to do an excellent job for one entity rather than a half -*ss one for two bosses. Kevin and I launched the criminal justice program and saw it through its first year. We both resigned in 2010 to pursue other professional avenues.

Barbara and I took more cruises in 2010 and I had been to Cozumel, Mexico so many times that I was thinking about running for mayor. I also went back to work for our local school district and got reconnected with the Knights of Columbus at the church. I had joined the Knights in 2008, but was not able to participate while I worked at Kaplan.

I continued to work for Mansfield ISD, go on cruises and attend the college graduation of our grandson Casey in 2011. From January through the end of the school year in June, I worked nearly every day. By this time, I had and still have several teachers who were now using me as their preferred substitute and it was great getting to work with and to know some of the kids. One of the major draw backs about substituting is that you really don't get to know the students as well as the full-time teachers do. I owe a big thank you to the second grade teachers at Louise Cabaniss Elementary for all of the assignments they gave me that school year and to Cleta Yancy and Brandie Mitchell whom I mentioned earlier.

The highlight of 2011 was attending the graduation ceremonies of our grandson. Casey Scott Butler graduated from Springhill College in Mobile, Alabama with honors in May of 2011. Casey had also been selected to attend medical school at the University of Oklahoma (OU) and has just recently started his third year of training. He wants to be a surgeon. I am quite sure that he will do very well. I sent him a text message about something the other day and I was delighted with his reply. He said I will call you when I get out of the OR. I thought that's pretty cool. Casey has inherited his charm and stunning good looks from his Pop and his brains from his mom and dad.

After Casey's graduation, Barbara and I took seven young people (Casey, Michael, Jessica, Josh and three friends of Michael's from Georgia Tech) to Orlando for a week at our time share. We got them two day tickets to Universal Studios and just turned them loose on their own. They all seemed to have a good time and Barbara and I were really worn out by weeks' end.

Barbara and I also went on three cruises in 2011. We had big time fun on all of them. Barbara now remembers to take medications for all circumstances, since her ship's doctor experience on our first cruise when she was placed in quarantine. We sailed by ourselves in February with Lee, Claudia and Dave and Lori Tomlin in May. Then again, with Gary and Kathy in November. The November trip was really nice as we returned to Nassau. We had the opportunity to spend some more time with my good friend Mario. As always, Mario gave us his car for the day and we were able to take Gary and Kathy all over the island. We all lost a little money in the casino at the Atlantis, but all in all had a really great day in Nassau.

The year 2011 ended just like every other year has ended since with moved to Mansfield, as we spent New Year's Eve with Lee and Claudia and all of our good friends from church. This was and is one of the things that I have come to look forward to every year. Lee actually stays awake past 9pm. We also get to feast on Claudia's great chili.

I would be elected to my first officer position with the Knights of Columbus, continue teaching, give Jessica away and cruise some more in 2012. Barbara and I, along with Joan and Chris Heath, began the year by going on a Super Bowl cruise in February. Barbara and I had received two free cruises when we upgraded our time share. We invited Joan and Chris to join us. They had never cruised before and took in all of the sights of Cozumel and Progresso, Mexico. We also had a great time on the ship on Super Bowl Sunday, as there were tailgate parties everywhere. I think I saw every jersey from every team during the cruise, even though there were only two teams playing.

I was elected to the Chancellor position in my council of the Knights of Columbus in June and served in it for that fraternal year. It was a great year. Our council was able to exceed all of our goals.

On March 24, 2012 I cried like a big sissy baby when I had the honor of giving my granddaughter Jessica away to her new husband. She has and will always have a very special place in my heart and we have always been best buds. I lost it big time when the judge said, "Who gives this woman to this man?"

Jessica and Josh make a great couple and they are very much in love, but she was on that day and always will be my little princess. I gave her a nickname that I still use even today, but I am the only person on the planet that is allowed to use it. When Jessica was a baby and just starting to walk, her mom dressed her up in the frilliest dresses along with what I referred to as fancy pants. She was a baby, so she wore diapers, rubber pants and these frilly things which made her butt stuck out. She waddled like a duck. Remember, I am the expert on ducks since my days with Tom. With her permission, I will tell you that I have always and will continue to call her "Duckbutt" or "Duckie" when I am in a hurry.

Jessica and Josh live in Atlanta, so we don't get to

see them as often as we would like. I also had another great year with the local school district and substituted almost every day. Teachers are now, with my permission, just plugging me in when they need me. I block out days when I will not be available, but get scooped up on most days when I am free. It's great and I love it. It, also, keeps me out of Barbara's hair and away from her honey-do list.

My 72 year journey through "Curve Balls from Above" is coming to an end, as we are now in the current year of 2013. So far, this year, we have continued to work, gone on one of our best cruises ever and attended another grandson's college graduation and the year is only half over.

In May, our second grandson, Michael Robert Butler II (MR2), graduated with honors from Georgia Tech University. Barbara and I drove to Atlanta and along with the rest of the family attended his graduation. Michael is taking the MCAT and will be applying to medical schools when he gets his results back. He is going to follow in his big brother's footsteps. Like Casey, he has also inherited his charm and extremely handsome features from his grandfather and his brain power from his mom and dad.

From January through June, Barbara and I continued to work for the local school district. Barbara does aide work, is really good at it and likes working almost as much as I do. Now that she is also working, I am having a tough time coming up with excuses for not doing things around the house. I am now expected to do a little more.

The last "Curve Ball" from above, that I will write about, occurred the week after we returned from Michael's graduation. Barbara and I had reservations to sail to Bermuda in June to celebrate our 50th wedding anniversary, but the ship we were to sail on caught fire in the Bahamas. All cruises on that ship were cancelled from then until mid-July, which would be long after our wedding anniversary.

Remember, Barbara graduated from high school in Bermuda, so we had made arrangements for lunches and dinners with some of her friends during the time we would be in port there.   She and I were both disappointed, as we both love Bermuda. This would be the first time we would have gone there by ship.

Those special "Guiding Forces" in our lives kicked it into high gear and made our 50th anniversary one we will always remember and cherish.   Royal Caribbean was very understanding and accommodating and we were able to sail on the Oasis of the Seas out of Fort Lauderdale, Florida. We didn't know it at the time of the booking, but the Oasis is the largest cruise ship in the world. It is like sailing on your own island or town. It has everything on it that you could imagine or want. The cruise line also upgraded us from an ocean view cabin to a superior balcony suite and gave some money back. We also got an upgrade on our next booking with them. What a deal! We were so pleased that we have booked another cruise for Valentine's Day next year and have persuaded Lee and Claudia to join us. Their wedding anniversary will happen while we are this cruise, so they will get a two- fer.

We drove from Mansfield to Fort Lauderdale and really took our time about it. Poor Tequila was at the vet for almost two weeks. We stopped the first night in Crestview, Florida near Eglin AFB and seeing all the short hair cuts made me a little homesick for my old Air Force days. On the second day, we drove over to Orlando and visited with some good friends we knew from our tours of duty in the Bahamas. It was really great seeing Rick and Ester. They took us out for some of the best catfish that I have had in a while.

On Friday, we drove to Fort Lauderdale, and spent some time with a friend we knew from our days in Miami. Patty and her mom treated us to dinner at a casino and we all won some money that I would donate back on the ship.

On Saturday, we boarded the Oasis and sailed to Nassau, St Thomas and St Martin. We scratched these sites off our bucket lists. Since our return from the cruise, we have used our pool almost every day, Barbara has tried to get me to do things I don't want to do, and life goes on.

Me and My Beautiful Barbara Celebrating 50 Years Together

It is my sincerest hope that you have enjoyed reading about the first 72 years of my life as much as I have had recalling and writing about it. I am so excited that I am starting a book on the second 72 years, but don't have a title just yet. I have no idea when I might have decided to put all of my thoughts on paper, but I am very happy that I have. There are things and people that I have written about that I have not thought about in years. It felt and feels good to have made this journey. Barbara has read almost all of what I have written and has commented about how much she has learned about me that she didn't know already. Remember, we have been married for 50 years. We have always been very close, but I think that we are ever closer now than we have ever been.

I hope that you have enjoyed *Curve Balls from Above* enough to look for book two in 72 years from now. I have been amused and enlightened by it. I also hope that all of the people I have written about will forgive me and that they have the fond memories I do of all of them. I would, also, hope that you have learned or at least thought about some of the things that have happened in your lives and have the same kind of feeling that I have about mine. There is one thing that I think I have learned or at least brought out of the cobwebs in my brain. It is that from this day forward when I wake up in the morning, I am going to approach the new day with the attitude that "This is the very first day of the rest of my life" and live it to the fullest. I am going to try to show my appreciation to my God, my country, my family and my friends for all that I have and what they all mean to me.

Butch